## Robert Boyle
Trailblazer of Science

Robert Boyle lived a life of contrasts. He was born to one of the richest families on earth, but he chose to live a simple life. Robert became one of the greatest scientists of all time, but remained a shy, humble person. Despite his quiet nature, he worked forcefully and bravely against persecution and injustice. Robert Boyle's friends were a roll call of the famous: Christopher Wren, Samuel Pepys, John Milton, Isaac Newton and many others. Yet, during his life Robert Boyle towered over all of them.

Robert's brothers and sisters all received regal titles such as knight, viscount, earl, lord. However, Robert Boyle refused all titles. He preferred to remain what he was, a Christian gentleman.

Robert Boyle's father came to Ireland with nothing but a few coins in his pocket and a small trunk of clothes. He became the Great Earl of Cork, a powerful and wealthy Irish landowner.

Like his father, Robert Boyle became famous, but in an entirely different way. He became the best known and most respected scientist of his day. Today, after three hundred years, he is still considered one of the top scientists of all time.

Robert Boyle survived rebellions in Ireland, the English Civil War, the Black Death, the Great Fire and political unrest. He succeeded in making many remarkable discoveries during those difficult times. He lived a devout Christian life, using his science to glorify God. Read *Robert Boyle — Trailblazer of Science* to experience these exciting events.

## ABOUT THE AUTHOR

John Hudson Tiner has been a science teacher, mathematician, and a cartographer (map maker). He is the author of more than twenty books. "I especially like to write biographies of famous people of the past," he says. "After I finish the research, a magic moment occurs when the story takes over. The characters come alive. No longer am I a writer. I become a time traveler who stands unseen in the shadows and reports the events as they take place."

Mr. Tiner is well known for his popular books about science and religion. Other Sowers Series books by Mr. Tiner include biographies of *Isaac Newton, Johannes Kepler, Samuel F.B. Morse,* and *Louis Pasteur.* He is also the author of *When Science Fails*, published by Baker Books, and several science textbooks.

John Hudson Tiner and wife, Jeanene, live in High Ridge, Missouri. They have two children, John Watson and Lambda.

## ABOUT THE ARTIST

Michael L. Denman says he has always liked to draw. He remembers that in his poor family paper was scarce. So his grandmother gave him her Christmas cards, which in those days were always folded into fourths. Michael unfolded them and was delighted to have full sheets of paper, blank on one side, ready for his drawings. His favorite books as a child were those on history, so he especially likes to illustrate history books for today's children. He read this book before illustrating it and was fascinated to see where science was at in the days of Robert Boyle. He noted that some areas of science were very advanced while some lagged, and he noted that people had great courage in those days to carry· on with everyday life. His 11-year-old daughter enjoyed reading the book too.

Mr. Denman at first learned most of his art skills by himself, but later he studied art at Cooper Institute. For more than ten years he has illustrated children's storybooks, workbooks and readers, as well as visual aids that teachers use. He is an Art Director at McCallum Design Company and lives with his wife and family in North Ridgeville, Ohio.

# Robert Boyle

## Trailblazer of Science

by

## John Hudson Tiner

illustrated by Michael L. Denman

MOTT
MEDIA

*This book is dedicated to*
*Karen*

COPYRIGHT © 1989 by Mott Media, Inc.

Kurt Dietsch, Cover Artist

LIBRARY OF CONGRESS CATALOGING IN PUBLICATION DATA

Tiner, John Hudson, 1944
    Boyle, Robert: Trailblazer of Science / by John Hudson Tiner.

    p.    cm.—(Sowers Series)
    Bibliography: p. 182
    Includes index.

    SUMMARY: A biography of the seventeenth-century Anglo-Irish scientist who, among his other accomplishments, is considered to be the founder of modern chemistry.
    ISBN 0-88062-155-9
    1. Boyle, Robert, 1627-1691—Juvenile literature. 2. Scientists—Great Britain—Biography—Juvenile literature.    [1. Boyle, Robert, 1627-1691. 2. Chemists. 3. Scientists.] I. Title. II. Series: Sowers.
Q143.B77T56    1989        530'.092'4—dc19 [B] [92]        89-3130
                                                            CIP AC

ISBN 0-88062-155-9    Paperbound

# CONTENTS

# 1

# The Great Earl of Cork

The scene is a green valley of Ireland in the fall of 1631. A mist covers the lower part of the valley. A chill is in the early morning air. Soon the sun will be higher and burn away the mist. Nestled in the valley is a small farmhouse with thick walls, tiny windows and a thatched roof. A poor peasant family lives in the house.

The peasant family has a visitor. His name is Robert Boyle, called Robyn. He is four-and-a-half years old. For most of his life Robyn has lived with the peasant family.

Robyn Boyle's father is one of the richest men in the world, and the most powerful man in Ireland.

This morning, Robyn Boyle could hardly contain his excitement. He was going home at last. He slipped into his simple, pull-over shirt. He hitched up his well-worn trousers and tied them with a canvas belt. Both shirt and trousers were made of homespun material.

Next he slipped into his shoes. They came from the local cobbler. Rapidly he wove the shoestrings around the hooks, tying them. Robyn ran his fingers through his hair. There, finished.

Robyn looked around the room he had shared with children of the peasant family. Against the far wall a cradle hung by ropes from the ceiling rafters. It rocked gently back and forth. For two years Robyn had slept there. He could remember resting in the cradle, watching the shadows of the fireplace flicker across the ceiling.

Should he take anything with him? He shook his head. No, nothing here belonged to him. He liked this house, but for as long as Robyn could remember, he'd been told that his place would be with his father at Lismore Castle. Tonight, he would be cozy and warm in his father's castle. He would see his brothers and sisters. He would hug his mother and sit in his father's lap. He would take his place as the seventh son of the Great Earl of Cork.

The farmer's wife looked him over critically. "Clean clothes, clean hands and face. You have a good complexion and strong body. The Great Earl will be happy with what he sees."

"I'm ready," Robyn said, speaking carefully. He scarcely trusted his voice. He tended to stammer when he became excited.

The woman said, "Robyn, eat your breakfast. You'll leave my home with a full stomach." She looked fondly at the little boy. He was such a sweet child, and she found it difficult to treat him merely as a guest. However, the Great Earl insisted that she and Robyn not become attached to one another.

Robyn sat down at the table. He said his prayers quickly and began eating the meal. The breakfast could not have been simpler. He ate boxty, a type of potato pancake, a bowl of hot oatmeal, and a cup of buttermilk.

Robyn asked, "Do my brothers live away from home, too?"

The farmer's wife said, "Yes, when they were young like you. Your father doesn't like to bring his sons up so nice and tenderly that a hot sun or a good shower of rain would damage you, as if you were made of butter or sugar. He thinks hardships in the early years will help you appreciate the good things as you grow older."

"What about my sisters?" Robyn asked as he spooned up the last of the oatmeal.

The woman said, "The girls stay home until a marriage is arranged for them. When they're twelve years old or so, they go to live with the families of their future husbands."

Robyn had spent the first six months of his life at Lismore, being raised by a nursemaid, before leaving home. He could not remember his mother. However, the Great Earl had come to the peasant's house several times a year to be with his son. Once, the Great Earl took Robyn on a two-week trip through Ireland. Robyn rode in the saddle with his father, held snugly in his father's arms. The Great Earl was always doing something exciting and interesting. Robyn could hardly wait to go home to be with him.

After Robyn finished breakfast, the woman walked outside with him. She wrapped a blanket around his shoulders because of the chill. The path from the cottage passed through a thick hedgerow and opened onto a winding road. Deep ruts from the passage of countless wagons and carts cut into the narrow road. The road twisted around hills and valleys, following the easiest route.

A man with a donkey cart waited for Robyn. He

had agreed to let Robyn ride with him to a nearby village. One of the Great Earl's servants would meet Robyn there and take him home to Lismore Castle.

Robyn climbed into the cart. He turned around and waved goodbye. For a passing moment Robyn felt a lump in his throat as the woman waved back. She turned and walked away.

At first Robyn rode in the back of the cart with his legs dangling. The ride became so rough it jarred his teeth. He climbed to the front to sit on a bag of oats.

An unseen dog barked in the distance. An impatient cow mooed, wanting to be milked. A flock of ducks waddled out of a barnyard on their way to a pond. They all quacked at once, as if in a deep argument.

At the village, the servant sent by the Great Earl met them. He was an ageless man; small, patient, and soft-spoken. A silent and bored driver waited to click into action the team of horses pulling the carriage. A footboy about twelve years old rode at the back of the carriage on a running board.

The servant smiled in welcome. He said, "My name is Carew." He lifted the soiled and smelly blanket from Robyn Boyle's shoulders. Carew held it by thumb and forefinger and dropped it into the donkey cart. Carew instructed the man in the donkey cart, "Please return this to its owner."

To Robyn, Carew said, "I'll dress you in proper clothes at the castle. In the meantime, you may wear this." He placed a cloak around Robyn's shoulders. The cloak was the finest and most expensive garment Robyn had ever worn.

The footboy quickly jumped down and placed portable steps by the carriage so Robyn and Carew could climb aboard. Robyn sank back in the padded bench. The carriage swayed into motion. Robyn marveled at how smooth it felt compared to the bone-jarring ride of the donkey cart.

Robyn asked many questions about what to expect at the castle. He found that Carew needed only a little prompting. The man enjoyed talking, especially about the Great Earl of Cork.

Carew said, "The Great Earl of Cork is a man of endless energy. He came to Ireland from England. He landed at Dublin with only 27 pounds in cash and a few clothes. Starting with those humble belongings he has risen to the greatest landowner in Ireland, and the richest Englishman."

Although the carriage offered a smoother ride, it traveled not much faster than the donkey cart. They were still on the road at noon. Robyn grew hungry. He asked Carew if they were going to eat.

Carew said, "Your father has planned a great banquet to welcome you home. It will be a fancy feast with more food than you'll be able to eat. However, I did pack a light meal for you."

From the other seat the servant turned back a blanket which covered a wicker basket. Inside the basket was a pie made of bacon, hard-boiled eggs and mashed potatoes baked in bread. The food was delicious and quite unlike anything Robyn had eaten before. There was fresh fruit, and cider to drink.

As they neared Lismore, Robyn Boyle noticed greater activity along the way. They passed a crew of men working on the road. The men stopped to wave as the carriage passed. They rode over a new bridge. Upstream, a water wheel creaked as the rushing current turned it.

Carew said, "Some English landowners see how much they can take out of Ireland. Most native Irishmen resent their English landlords. The Great Earl is different. He puts the greater part of his profits

back into his estates. Your father has done much to improve the trade and industry of the area. He has established schools and houses for the poor. He laid out roads and constructed bridges. He founded a number of factories and towns.''

Robyn could certainly see his father's hand upon the land. He saw improvements everywhere he looked. In the distance, a tall chimney discharged a thick cloud of smoke.

Carew said, ''The smoke is from the furnace in the ironworks.''

Later that afternoon the carriage topped a rise and Robyn glimpsed Lismore. Even in the distance it looked impressive. Flags flew from turrets that towered over the stone walls. The Great Earl had fortified the castle, making it a stronghold. The terraced gardens and grass-covered earthen fortifications made it less forbidding than most castles.

They crossed the Blackwater river and pulled into the grounds of Lismore Castle. Workmen swarmed everywhere around the estate.

''What is happening?'' Robyn asked. He saw carpenters, masons and gardeners at work.

''The Great Earl is rebuilding Lismore to make it the noblest house in the province of Munster.'' Carew pointed here and there, naming the construction in process: ''He's building stables and coach houses, pigeon houses and fish ponds. The wall around the orchard and gardens is nearly finished. Over there are the liveries for the coachmen and footmen. They've demanded better living quarters now that the castle is so much improved.''

Robyn and Carew stepped down from the carriage at the front entrance. Carew spoke to a servant, who took Robyn's hand and led him inside. ''Your father rode out this morning with a hunting party and will be back shortly. We'll have plenty of time to prepare you to meet him. You must make a good impression."

Carew walked Robyn rapidly through the castle.They passed by rooms filled with furniture of crimson velvet, fringed with white lace. Tapestry hung on the walls. Turkish rugs spread over the floors. Intricate embroideries rested on high-backed chairs.

"This is your room," Carew said finally. "Let's get you out of these clothes and into ones more suitable for the seventh son of the Great Earl of Cork."

Robyn looked around his room. A great canopied bed hung with purple cloth dominated the room. Carved wooden fretwork covered the ceiling. The walls were painted in Spanish white.

Robyn finished removing his peasant clothes. Carew's look of disgust left little doubt about what would happen to them. He would dump them with the garbage.

Carew laid out Robyn's new clothes on the bed and helped Robyn dress. The underclothes were ordinary looking. All the outer clothes were lavish and decorated with ribbons. Robyn slipped into his soft, deerskin boots. They reached to the knees and turned down. A doublet, a close-fitting sleeveless outer vest, completed the outfit.

A few minutes later, a servant announced the return of the Great Earl. Carew walked with Robyn to the Great Earl's study. He led Robyn into the room. Then Carew backed out, leaving Robyn alone with his father.

The Great Earl's face broke into a broad smile. He held out his hands in welcome. "Give me a hug!" his voice boomed out.

Robyn ran over and climbed into his father's lap. The Great Earl hugged him and held him.

The Great Earl dipped a quill pen in ink and

finished writing an entry in a large book on his desk. He said, "In this ledger I record not only my business activities, but everything else of importance that happens. I regard myself a lucky man. As a young man I came to Ireland to seek my fortune. The blessings of God enriched my estate. I need not envy any of my neighbors. The wealth of a man is in his family."

He turned the pages of the journal. The writing was in a very tight, precise hand. "Here is where I recorded the birth of my first child, Roger. He was born at Youghal in 1606. He died nine years later." He stopped on another page. "Your oldest sister, Alice, was born a year later, then Sarah, Lettice and Joan." He turned some more pages. "In 1612 Richard was born. He is the viscount of Dungarvan. Catharine is next. She will marry the viscount Ranelagh. Jeoffry died at birth. But Lewis, the second Roger, Mary, Francis and Margaret are healthy children."

"Am I in your book?" Robyn asked.

The Great Earl said, "Indeed you are." He found the place in the journal. "You were born here at Lismore about three o'clock in the afternoon on January 25, 1627. Here I record the birth of my seventh son and my fourteenth child. *God bless him, for his name is Robert Boyle.*"

The Great Earl closed the book. "I wanted to keep you from the dangers of too much ease and luxury. Are you happy to be back home?"

Suddenly, great emotion swept over Robyn. He began "I . . ."

Robyn sputtered to a stop. He hugged his father, hanging on tightly. Under normal circumstances, Robyn spoke with a slight stammer, which he did his best to overcome. When feelings were strong or when under stress, the stammer became more noticeable.

His father noticed the stammer and asked how Robyn acquired it.

Robyn said, "At the house where I lived, some of the children stammered. I made fun of them by doing it too."

The Great Earl of Cork finished the thought for him. "What you imitated in jest, came to be learned in earnest."

Robyn nodded miserably. "Now I stammer."

"What have you learned from this unfortunate event?" his father asked.

Robyn Boyle wrinkled his forehead in thought. "I shouldn't make fun of the misfortunes of others, or the same misfortune may befall me."

The Great Earl nodded wisely. "You're a smart lad for your age. You've learned a valuable lesson. Many people speak without thinking. Others speak in fits of anger. Later they regret their words. The stammer has taught you self control. You'll think before you speak. When you do speak, you'll be sure of yourself, else the stammer will return."

Many people assumed that Robyn Boyle was unusually shy. Actually, he didn't like talking to strangers because he feared he might start to stammer and embarrass himself.

He did not look forward with pleasure to the banquet that night. There would be so many strangers present. Robyn hardly knew any of the people. Here were his own brothers and sisters, yet he didn't know who was who.

Carew came to his rescue. He stood at Robyn's side and whispered their names in Robyn's ear. Robyn greeted each of them properly.

Robyn's mother wasn't at the banquet. Robyn hadn't seen her yet. He assumed she was with Margaret, his baby sister.

The Great Earl led the prayer. "The great God of heaven I do humbly beseech to bless all my children with long and religious lives. May they be fruitful and virtuous children and continue till their lives end loyal subjects of the King. May they prove themselves good patriots of the commonwealth."

Servants carried in silver trays stacked high with food. The Great Earl's banquet table soon filled with trays of fish and meats. Robyn tried to sample it all. He tasted plum preserves spread on oaten cakes, rich butter on hot rolls, strips of beef and venison in sauces. Everything smelled good. Finally, he finished eating and sat back to listen to the musicians. They played flutes, lutes, and other stringed instruments.

That night as Robyn went to sleep, he could not help but think about how much his life had changed. He had awakened this very morning in a narrow straw pallet resting on a dirt floor. Now he drifted off to sleep in a high canopied bed with feather mattress and thick, warm blankets. This morning he ate a simple breakfast from crude wooden bowls. Tonight he ate venison from silver plates. He started the journey home in a donkey cart. He finished the journey in a fancy carriage drawn by a sleek team of horses.

One puzzling thought remained. Why hadn't his mother come to say goodnight to him? But soon Robyn drifted off to sleep, warm and comfortable in the deep feather bed.

The next morning the Great Earl came to walk with him to the breakfast table. Robyn asked, "Where is mother?"

The Great Earl took him by the hand and sat down with him before the fireplace. As the wood crackled, the Great Earl said, "She was translated from this life into a better one on the 16th of February in 1630."

"She isn't here?" Robyn asked.

The Great Earl spoke in plain language. "She became ill shortly after the birth of Margaret. She died in Dublin about a year ago."

The Great Earl continued to speak, almost as if he were talking to himself. "Lady Boyle, your mother, was a most religious, virtuous, loving and obedient wife to me all the days of her life."

Robyn Boyle could hardly hear the words. He tightly held his father's hand. Tears streamed from his eyes. He tried to remember his mother. She must have held him in her arms. She must have spoken to him and kissed him. He'd been sent away at such a young age. He couldn't recall even the faintest memory of her.

He would never know her. It was as if a little bit of the joy had gone out of his life.

Robyn Boyle didn't meet all of his brothers and sisters until the fall of 1634. The Great Earl called home his sons and daughters for a family reunion at Lismore. All five of his sons made plans to be there, as did most of his eight daughters. Richard Boyle, the viscount of Dungarvan and the oldest of the Boyle boys, lived in England with his wife. The young Lord and Lady had been married for several months. This would be her first visit to Lismore.

Robyn traveled with his father to Dublin, Ireland's largest and best-known city. The Great Earl owned a townhouse in that city. While in Dublin, Robyn paid his respects to the grave site of his mother. She was buried at St. Patrick's church in a burial vault provided by her family, the Fentons. Robyn's grandfather, Sir Geoffry Fenton, had been the Secretary of State of Ireland. He was buried there, too.

Members of the Boyle family who sailed from England met at Dublin for the overland journey to Lismore. The Great Earl led the procession. The sons, daughters and in-laws were accompanied by attendants, servants, coachmen, footboys, and an escort of experienced horsemen.

Traveling was slow and difficult. The two-hundred mile journey from Dublin to Lismore took four days on the road. They spent the nights in the homes of friends along the way.

On the fourth day they prepared to cross Four Mile Waters. Normally, this brook could be easily forded. However, it had become swollen to a torrent by several days of heavy rains.

Robyn rode in an open carriage. A coachman rode at the front and a footman stood on a running board at the back.

The carriage driver hesitated at the edge of the roaring stream. As he did, the boy on the back of the coach jumped off. The stream proved much swifter and deeper than anybody expected. The roaring water caught the carriage. It shifted sideways. The coachman jumped free. They abandoned Robyn to the roaring stream.

A gentleman on horseback splashed into the swirling water. The rider reached over and grabbed Robyn by the collar. He carried Robyn to the other side.

The violent water hurtled the horses and carriage down the stream. The carriage overturned. The horses were caught in the rigging. They couldn't break free. One of them gave a frightened neigh. The other snorted water from its nose as it fought the current.

The Great Earl of Cork urged his horse into the water. He drew his sword. "Cut the harness loose!" he cried. His sword flashed as he hacked away at the leather harness. After much struggling, the horses broke their harness. The frightened animals swam to the opposite bank. The carriage tumbled downstream, breaking into pieces.

Robyn observed all of this while sitting in the saddle

with the man who had rescued him. He shivered as he looked at the turbulent water. He certainly would have drowned if he'd stayed in the coach.

"Are you all right, son?" the Great Earl asked.

Robyn summoned more courage than he actually felt. "Yes. This man pulled me from the carriage just in time. He saved me."

The Great Earl had another explanation. He said, "You've been placed in heaven's care by my prayers. Providence watched over you."

That night the Great Earl recorded the event in his journal. The water overthrew the coach. His son was rescued at the last possible moment. His horses were in danger of drowning. But . . . "We all, God be praised, arrived safely at Lismore."

Despite the size of his family, the Great Earl took an interest in each child. For instance, Lady Dungarvan, Richard Boyle's wife, was expecting a child. Earlier that year, when the orchard had bloomed so gloriously, the Great Earl promised to her the plums from a certain tree in his orchard.

A stone wall enclosed the orchard. An iron gate, which the Great Earl kept locked, guarded the entrance. Robyn's father gave him the key to the orchard gate. Robyn carried the key on a ribbon around his neck. He could enter the orchard anytime he wanted.

Robyn often went to the orchard to pick fruit. He ate it on the spot. He carefully refrained from eating too much. He wanted the fruit to remain a special treat.

One day as he walked through the garden, he came upon a tree filled with plums. He began eating them one by one. He enjoyed them far more than any dessert. He meant to eat only two or three plums. Before he knew it, he'd popped ten of them into his mouth.

Suddenly Robyn remembered that his father had promised these plums to Lady Dungarvan. Robyn raced from the orchard. He slammed the gate and locked it. Maybe no one had seen him eating the forbidden fruit.

Too late! Catharine, his seventeen-year-old sister, spied him from an upper window. She rushed to tell her father about the incident.

Catharine said, "I told Robyn your strict order to save the plums for Lady Dungarvan. He ate half a dozen of them."

The Great Earl of Cork summoned Robyn. "Is this true what your sister says," he demanded.

Robyn Boyle objected, "No it isn't true."

His sister looked at him aghast. "You deny eating those plums?"

"I deny eating six of them," Robyn said. "I ate ten plums!"

His father gave a sudden roar of laughter. He swooped down, picked up the boy and gave him a big hug. "How delightful to have a son who regards honesty so highly."

Robyn Boyle learned the importance of honesty. His absolute honesty became one of his most enduring traits. When it came time in later life to choose between truth and lies, he chose truth.

His father enjoyed telling the plum story to his friends to illustrate Robyn's truthful character. "Robyn is an enemy to a lie. He'd rather accuse himself of another fault, than to be suspected guilty of lying."

Even Catharine laughed at the story. The two children of the Great Earl grew especially fond of one another. Robyn Boyle became her favorite brother. He turned to her in times of trouble. In some ways Catharine became the mother he never knew.

# 2

# The Seventh Son

The Great Earl knew the importance of a good education. He even encouraged his daughters to learn to read and write. However, he lavished more care on improving Robyn's mind than upon the minds of any other of his children. Perhaps he saw that Robyn showed the greatest promise.

People say that a father bestows his greatest wealth on his oldest son but his greatest affection on his youngest son. In the case of the Great Earl and Robyn, that saying was true. The Great Earl took care to further Robyn's education. During his travels, the Great Earl would look for books that he thought would help Robyn. He would buy the books and send them back to Lismore Castle.

The Great Earl of Cork kept a close watch on his far-flung empire. He would leave home for several days to tour his estate. Robyn always wanted to go along.

"Can I go with you?" Robyn asked.

"First, attend to your studies," his father said. "If

Mr. Badnedge judges them satisfactory, you can go with me on the spring tour.'' The Great Earl employed Thomas Badnedge as a business manager and confidential secretary. Thomas Badnedge attended to the day-to-day details of the Great Earl's business.

Robyn threw himself into his studies. He did have an advantage over other students. Most schools assigned several students to each teacher. In Robyn's case, the Great Earl assigned several teachers to one student.

''French is the language spoken by lawyers and court officials,'' the Great Earl explained. ''I have hired a French tutor to instruct you in that language. Latin serves as the language of scholars. Mr. Wilkerson will teach you Latin.'' Mr. Wilkerson conducted worship services at the private chapel at Lismore. He served as the Great Earl's personal chaplain.

Robyn studied the Bible, too. A person who claimed to be well educated had to show a thorough knowledge of Scripture. Robyn read the King James Version of the Bible. This first major English translation appeared about 30 years earlier, in 1611.

Learning from textbooks alone did not entirely prepare a person to be a gentleman. Carew took a hand in the boy's education, too. Carew taught Robyn the finer points of royal etiquette.

Carew also taught Robyn practical skills such as horseback riding. ''If you are to travel with your father, you must learn how to handle a horse,'' Carew told Robyn.

The Great Earl had already celebrated his 65th birthday. Despite his age, Robyn knew that his father preferred to travel by horseback in spite of his age.

Carew explained why. ''Bad weather often closes the roads except to riders on horseback. Carriages

become mired in mud. Heavy rains wash out roads
entirely. Your father must travel in all kinds of
weather. He's a member of the Irish parliament.
Parliament sometimes holds sessions right after New
Year's, when winter weather is at its worst. The Great
Earl simply can't stay home when the roads turn to
mud.''

Robyn remembered the last-minute escape from
Four Mile Waters. The horses forded the stream but
the carriage didn't.

At the start of spring, Thomas Badnedge reviewed
Robyn's progress. He reported to the Great Earl.
''Robyn has made remarkable progress in his studies.
He can speak French and Latin. He has learned to
read English and write a fair hand.''

''Then he may go with me on the spring tour,''
the Great Earl agreed.

The spring tour kept the Great Earl of Cork and
his son in the saddle for eight days. They traveled
through the counties of Cork and Waterford and on
to Youghal harbor. They didn't ride by themselves.
A half dozen of the Earl's employees accompanied
them.

His father told Robyn about his early days in
Ireland. He described how he made his fortune. ''I
landed in Ireland as merely Richard Boyle, an
Englishman. I had a few coins in my pocket and the
clothes I carried with me,'' the Great Earl recalled.
''In a short time my fortunes turned for the better.
Sir Walter Raleigh owned 42,000 acres of good land
in Cork and Waterford. His ill-fated efforts in the New
World left his Irish holdings in disarray. He managed
them so poorly they actually drained money from his
treasury. I persuaded Sir Walter Raleigh to sell his
land to me. I improved it and made it prosper.''

Robyn could see that his father's efforts helped the

people who lived on his lands. They certainly fared better than those who lived on lands owned by other Englishmen. Robyn and his father rode outside the Great Earl's domain. The poverty became more evident. They passsed small rundown farms, old barns dark and sagging, and a few horses grazing.

The Great Earl said, "I'm writing the story of my life. I call it *True Remembrances*." The Great Earl laughed. "I've let people read the unfinished manuscript. My friends tell me it is too astonishing to be true. But true it is."

After four days, Robyn and his father arrived at the seaport of Youghal. The Great Earl took a lot of pride in his harbor. It lay on the southeast of Ireland, perfectly situated for sailing to Bristol in England.

"Youghal is my own private harbor," the Great Earl said. "To show a profit, I must ship my products to markets in England and on the continent. I've strengthened the harbor against attack."

"Attack?" Robyn asked. "Who would attack the harbor?"

"On the day I sailed to Ireland to seek my fortune, English ships sighted the Spanish Armada. The Armada appeared to be invincible, and England was not prepared for war. People along the seacoast became frightened. Only bad winds, the tricky currents in the English channel and the heroic action of a few brave English sailors defeated the Spanish fleet."

Robyn objected, "The Spanish attacked a long time ago. Do you expect them to invade again?"

"No, but pirates do sail the Atlantic. They like Ireland's many hidden bays and inlets," the Great Earl said. "In 1628, while you lived with the peasant family, I set out from England with your mother and two sisters, Lettice and Joan. A 300-ton man-of-war chased us. We escaped. My footmen, attendants and horses followed in a barque, a slower square-rigged ship. The pirates captured the slower ship.''

The Great Earl pointed to bulwarks, watchtowers and cannons aimed out to sea. ''Youghal can withstand any attack, whether by pirates or a second Spanish invasion.''

Robyn pulled up his horse at the top of a hill that overlooked the harbor. A brisk wind whipped across the crest. The wind roared in his ears. His cloak flopped back and forth. Winds filled the sails of a ship in the bay. It set a course out of the harbor

The Great Earl said, ''The ship is the *Pilgrim*. I bought it from Sir Walter Raleigh along with his land. It and another ship, the *Ninth Whelp*, transport linen, wool, fur and other products to England for sale.''

The route back home passed through the mining district. Small mines, furnaces, forges and ironworks dotted the landscape.

The Great Earl said, ''I do my best to exploit the mineral deposits of Munster. My mines yield silver, copper, lead and iron.''

Woodcutters cut down great swaths of the forest. The Great Earl explained, ''They bake the lumber to change it into charcoal for use in the iron smelting furnaces.''

Teams of horses dragged the logs together. The horses snorted and labored under the load. The teamsters clicked their tongues and snapped the reins. They urged the teams to greater effort. Workmen stacked the logs and covered the stack with mud. The stack looked like a mud hut. Once the mud dried, a man thrust a torch into the wood, setting it afire.

The Great Earl said, ''The wood burns only partially. The heat bakes the rest, turning it into charcoal.''

Robyn picked up a piece of the black, porous

material. The charcoal crumbled in his hands.

"Charcoal helps refine iron from its ore," his father explained. They walked inside the ironworks. "We fill the furnace with charcoal and crushed iron ore. Then we heat it red hot and send a blast of air through the mixture."

Robyn saw the fiery blast from the furnace. He felt the heat upon his face. He watched fascinated as molten iron splattered into molds. Slowly the metal cooled into bars.

The Great Earl said, "The bars are cast iron, which is hard but brittle." The Great Earl struck the bar sharply with a hammer. The cast iron shattered.

"A sudden blow breaks it," the Great Earl explained. "We change cast iron into wrought iron by heating it with iron ore and limestone. Wrought iron is too soft to make weapons or tools. Instead, it is used for ornamental designs on fences and gates.

"Steel is somewhere between brittle cast iron and soft wrought iron. Making steel requires the utmost skill. The mix of cast iron, charcoal, iron ore and limestone must be exactly right."

They watched as a blacksmith heated a bar of steel. He hammered it into the shape of a sword. Then he heated the sword red hot. Quickly he quenched it in cold water. The water hissed. The blacksmith held up the sword and examined it. The surface of the metal shimmered with a blue luster.

The Great Earl said, "The sudden plunge of hot steel into cold water improves it. The process tempers the steel, making it even stronger and harder."

"Why is that?" Robyn asked.

"I certainly do not know," the Great Earl admitted. "My experts tell me that iron has been forged in this way since ancient biblical times. The method works, which is all anyone understands."

The visit to the ironworks awakened in Robyn an interest in chemistry, the study of matter and how to change it from one form to another.

Robyn returned to his books. His studious nature endeared him very much to his father. The Great Earl became more and more convinced that he had a remarkable youngest son.

The summer of 1635 ended four years of private tutoring at home. The Great Earl called in Thomas Badnedge. The Great Earl said, "I've arranged for each of my other sons to inherit estates and be made viscounts, dukes and earls. They will become military leaders, politicians and businessmen. Robyn shows no interest in acquiring wealth or collecting titles.''

Thomas Badnedge agreed. ''He needs a better education than Ireland can provide.''

Thoughtfully, the Great Earl said, ''It is time for Robyn to leave home again. If wealthy families bring up their children entirely at home, the children are tempted into pride and idleness.''

''Robyn is unlikely to become lazy and a lover of luxuries,'' Thomas Badnedge pointed out.

The Great Earl dismissed that objection. ''The boy needs the discipline of a good boarding school in England.''

''Eton?'' Thomas Badnedge suggested. Eton was the famous English boarding school in Windsor near London.

''Yes,'' the Great Earl said. ''Eton is the perfect choice. Sir Henry Wotton is the provost. We are old friends. I have known him for many years. He's not only a fine gentleman himself, but he's very well skilled in the art of making others so.''

The Great Earl knew that his son wanted to stay home. He broke the news to Robyn as easily as he could. ''I've arranged for Sir Henry Wotton to oversee your education. You'll like him. Sir Henry has served as ambassador to Italy and other European countries. He has many interesting stories to tell.''

Robyn tried to keep his dismay from his face. He tried to please his father, whom he loved. Yet . . .

''I don't want to leave home again,'' Robyn wailed.

The Great Earl wrapped Robyn in his arms. ''You'll not be alone. Frank will attend Eton, too.''

Robyn brightened. Francis Boyle, known as Frank, was Robyn's older brother by two and a half years.

The personalities of Robyn and Frank complemented one another. Frank was bold and made friends easily. Robyn was more reserved. Frank

enjoyed outside activities and found it difficult to study. Robyn put his studies first. Frank always noticed what was happening around him. Robyn often lost himself in thought.

People described Frank as a sweet boy. He was a dependable, friendly boy. Frank seemed perfectly fearless and completely at ease in his role as one of the Great Earl of Cork's sons.

On September 9, 1635, Robyn and Frank, with Carew their personal servant, left Lismore for Youghal harbor. Thomas Badnedge accompanied them. He carried the money, 50 pounds. The Great Earl also gave each of the boys a parting gift of three pounds.

The trip would take them across stormy St. George's Channel and into Bristol Channel. That night the Great Earl penned in his journal, "The great God in heaven, bless, guide and protect them!"

The little party didn't sail from Youghal right away. They waited a week for favorable winds. At last they sailed, only to be beaten back by a storm. Eight days passed. They boarded the Great Earl's own ship, the *Ninth Whelp*. This time they sailed successfully to Bristol.

From Bristol they traveled by coach to Eton. They arrived on October 2. The tedious trip of four hundred miles took almost a month. Finally, Thomas Badnedge delivered the two boys into the charge of Sir Henry Wotton.

Sir Henry Wotton led them to his home. He explained that they would stay with him for a while. "Your permanent chambers are being made ready in the home of Mr. John Harrison, the chief schoolmaster."

As they walked across the campus, Sir Henry Wotton described the school with obvious and honest pride. "Eton is two hundred years old. King Henry VI established it in 1440. Some of the scholars live in dormitories. Others stay in inns or homes of local residents."

At first, the layout of the campus presented a puzzling patchwork to Robyn. He feared he'd get lost merely going from one class to another. Soon he figured out the design. The school had been laid out as two squares, or quadrangles. Around the outer square stood the chapel, separate classroom buildings for freshmen and upperclassmen, and the long chamber, a dormitory. Buildings were of mellow red brick, except for the chapel which was of grey stone. Trees shaded the walks between the buildings. A smaller quadrangle, known as the cloisters, nested inside the larger quadrangle. Around the smaller square stood the library, dining hall, offices and the residences of Sir Henry Wotton and schoolmasters.

Robyn and Frank began their schooling in style. They lived at the very heart of the campus in the home of the provost of the school. The Great Earl's business manager arranged for the two boys to receive a generous allowance. If they ran short they could call upon Mr. Burlamachy, the Lord Mayor of London. The Great Earl had established a letter of credit with him. Mr. Burlamachy would provide funds in an emergency. Carew remained with the two boys. He would attend to them throughout their stay at Eton.

However, school officials expected as much from Robyn and Frank as they did from other students. The school supervised every aspect of their lives, including games and play time. In one way or another, students devoted every precious hour to improving their minds and bodies.

Very soon Robyn learned that a scholar's day began well before dawn. He arose at five thirty for morning devotions. After praying and reading from the Bible, he raced off to breakfast, followed by two hours of classes. Robyn studied Latin, the Bible, arithmetic, logic and history. Every once in a while he heard a special lecture in astronomy or natural science.

During the morning recess, most students played outside. Robyn stole away to his room to read. He loved to read. He devoured books on all subjects— classics, poetry, history, biographies, adventure and travel. With one ear he listened for the bell calling him to chapel. Morning chapel service was followed by the noon meal.

Robyn and Frank ate in the dining hall with the rest of the boarders. However, sons of royalty sat at a table reserved for them. Robyn and Frank shared the table with four sons of the Earl of Northhampton and two sons of the Earl of Peterborough.

Classes resumed after dinner and lasted until three.

Professors encouraged students to spend their afternoon break in out-of-door activity. Sports included hurling, rugby, cricket and rowing. Once again, Robyn mustered whatever excuse he could to avoid the playing fields.

Robyn's burning passion for knowledge raised a problem for Mr. Harrison, the headmaster. He didn't think Robyn got enough exercise.

One afternoon, John Harrison found Robyn reading in a hidden corner of the library.

The man came to Robyn and gave him a ball.

"Why are you giving this to me?" Robyn asked.

"I took it away from a boy who was playing with it when he should have been studying." John Harrison said. "I'm giving it to you because you're studying when you should be playing."

"I'd much rather be here than outside," Robyn said.

Mr. Harrison said, "I fear reading is capturing too much of your time. A boy can be too interested in schooling." He insisted that Robyn close his books and spend some time on the outside with the other boys.

Robyn loathed athletics. When forced into it, Robyn did take up tennis, but he never became good at it.

Another class followed the exercise hour. After the evening meal, with it growing dark outside, Robyn spent a few minutes in the library. He returned to his room to light candles for a couple of hours of reading.

At seven o'clock students ended their studies. They had an hour of free time and could eat a late snack if they wished. Robyn's day ended at eight o'clock. The tired scholar blew out the candles and climbed into bed.

Robyn took to his studies with real fervor. He possessed a sharp mind, a ready memory, and a strong desire to learn. These skills thrust him to the head of his class. He often did better than students older by two or three years.

Some students put too much importance upon their studies. They became "grinds." They studied out of a sense of duty or to show off. These students plunged into despair when they missed a question. Or, they became angry when outdone by others. Grinds seldom made many friends.

Despite his success as a scholar, Robyn never became a grind. Other students did not resent his good grades. Even those pupils who would rather have been somewhere else than in a classroom counted Robyn as a friend. Robyn did excel in his studies, but he did so out of sheer enthusiasm.

Robyn's professors taught by reading from the books of the ancient scholars. Robyn learned geometry from the books of Euclid, astronomy from Ptolemy, medicine from Galen and logic from Aristotle. These Greek and Roman writers lived more than two thousand years earlier. Students had to study from approved books. They also had to memorize the answers from them.

Sir Henry Wotton didn't completely agree with the way most schools taught science. "There is a way to learn about nature without resorting to a book," Sir Henry told Robyn.

Robyn asked, "A way of learning other than finding the answer in a book?" The idea completely mystified him.

Sir Henry Wotton said, "Come to dine with me tonight. We will discuss what I consider the most important idea of this century. I call it the *experimental method*."

# 3

# Experimental Science

Students at Eton liked Sir Henry Wotton. He would often stop to chat with them and encourage them. Sir Henry also invited them to dine with him in his home. He would invite a small group to each dinner. In this way he learned more about his students.

Robyn eagerly accepted the invitation to Sir Henry's home. He knew that Sir Henry had served the King for many years in foreign countries. Sir Henry counted princes, statesmen, artists and scientists as his friends. He filled his home with books, curios, paintings and other rare and interesting treasures.

In addition, Sir Henry held a burning interest in science, or natural philosophy. He kept up with the latest advances. He built a small chemical laboratory in his home. He distilled herbs to make perfume and lotions. He made everything from medicinal tonics to oils for spraying on lures to attract trout.

At the evening meal, Sir Henry talked about the great men of science. Sir Henry said, ''When I was in Europe, Galileo and Kepler were the best known and most successful natural philosophers. Galileo studied motions of bodies on earth. John Kepler studied the motion of bodies in the heavens.''

One of the students, a grind named Malcolm, used this chance to impress Sir Henry Wotton. ''Ptolemy teaches that the planets must travel at constant speed around circular orbits.''

''Yes, but Ptolemy's system needs more than 70 circles to completely describe how the planets go. John Kepler wanted to replace Ptolemy's complicated system with a simpler one. Working from the observations of the great Tycho Brahe, he plotted the orbit of Mars around the sun. He proved that the orbit isn't a circle, but rather an ellipse.''

From their studies, Robyn and the other boys knew that an ellipse is like an oval, only pointed at each end.

Sir Henry said, ''John Kepler showed that Mars' speed isn't constant, either. It travels faster when its orbit carries it closer to the sun. John Kepler summarized the complex motions of the planets with three simple laws. These laws swept away Ptolemy's confusing jumble of circles.

''By the time of John Kepler's death in 1630, astronomers hailed him as the greatest astronomer who ever lived. He showed that a few simple rules governed the motions of heavenly bodies.''

Sir Henry continued, ''While Kepler examined motions in the heavens, Galileo did the same for motions on earth. Galileo dropped weights from a height. He calculated the flight of projectiles shot from a cannon. He measured the speed of balls rolling down an incline. He showed that the ancient Greeks, especially Aristotle, weren't always right about the motions of bodies here on earth. Suppose an iron ball that weighs one hundred pounds falls from a height of one hundred cubits. Aristotle stated that it would reach the ground before a one-pound ball had fallen a single cubit. In other words, a ball one hundred times as heavy falls one hundred times as fast.''

Malcolm spoke, ''Isn't that true sir?''

Sir Henry explained, ''Rather than looking up the answer in one of Aristotle's books, Galileo did an experiment. He simply dropped iron balls of different sizes from the tower of Pisa.''

''Well,'' Robyn prompted, ''which struck the ground first?''

Sir Henry said, ''Why don't we repeat Galileo's experiment for ourselves?'' As he spoke, he removed two coins from his pocket. One was a small silver twopence, the other a gold sovereign.

Sir Henry said, "The gold coin weighs about 20 times as much as the silver twopence. I am going to drop the coins at the same time. Which one will strike the floor first?"

Malcolm answered promptly, "The heavier one, of course. Aristotle says so."

Sir Henry turned his hand over, releasing the coins. Robyn listened for the *plink* of the small coin and the *plunk* of the heavier one. Both coins hit the floor at precisely the same instance.

Sir Henry said, "When Galileo dropped the two different iron balls, both struck the ground at the same time, too. He proved Aristotle wrong. From his experiments, Galileo concluded that all bodies fall at the same speed.

"Excuse me, sir," Malcolm said. "Galileo can't be correct. Some objects do fall faster than others. Even the copper twopence falls faster than a feather."

Sir Henry waved his hand about, stirring air currents. The flame of a nearby candle flickered back and forth. Sir Henry said, "You are forgetting air resistance. Air is a substance. Its resistance affects lighter objects more than heavier ones. A feather falls slower because of the greater air resistance. Galileo predicted that both a feather and a coin dropped in a vacuum would fall side by side."

Malcolm objected, "A vacuum cannot exist."

Sir Henry said, "Aristotle teaches that nature abhors a vacuum. But if Aristotle is wrong about the speed of falling bodies, then he may be wrong about a vacuum, too."

Malcolm repeated stubbornly, "Making a vacuum is impossible."

Sir Henry said, "Maybe so. Neither Galileo nor any other natural philosopher has found a way to drop a coin and a feather in a vacuum."

"Isn't it improper to interfere with nature?" another boy objected. He quoted one of his instructors. " 'The proper role of a natural philosopher is to develop systems of thought from self-evident principles.' "

Sir Henry said, "Logic and observation are important, but they are not enough. A natural philosopher must sometimes take matters into his own hands. Experiments may be the only way to gather the facts necessary either to prove or disprove a theory. For instance, how long must one wait for two different coins to accidentally fall to the floor? Isn't it simpler to drop the coins intentionally and draw conclusions from that observation?"

Robyn nodded. As he looked around the table he saw only one or two other boys in agreement. Obviously, they felt that logic and a few everyday observations would get them to the bottom of any question.

Robyn accepted the experimental method as the way to study nature. He became impatient with many of his classes. Science teachers avoided experimentation and direct experience. Instead, they simply looked for answers in ancient books.

Sir Henry agreed that schools could improve their teaching methods. "Eton, however, is better than most. Here is a teaching manual from another school." He picked up the book and read from it. " 'The teacher is not to permit any new opinions or discussions to be put forward; nor to cite or allow others to cite the opinions of an author not of known repute.' "

Almost everyone accepted the classical authors as final authorities, even in medical schools. Doctors learned medicine from the books of Hippocrates and Galen.

Galen, who lived in A.D. 150 , made the first attempts to master anatomy. Doctors must know the structure of the human body. Anatomy is the study of the human body. The word *anatomy* is the Greek word meaning "to cut". One way to study anatomy is to cut or dissect a body to examine its parts. Galen dissected animals—dogs, goats, pigs and monkeys. He described what he saw in careful detail. Not everything he saw in the animals held true in the human body.

Galen wrote about 80 books. In them, he stated his discoveries with force and vigor. Those who came after him looked upon his books as the final say about anatomy.

Professors refused to waste their time with what they considered messy, time-consuming dissections. "Galen has described the human body perfectly," these professors said. "Dissections serve no purpose. Students can learn anatomy just as well by reading a book."

Hippocrates lived even earlier than Galen, about 400 B.C. Hippocrates taught that disease resulted from an imbalance of the vital fluids, or *humors*, of the body. Hippocrates wrote, "The body has in itself blood, phlegm, yellow bile and black bile. . . We enjoy perfect health when these elements are in the right proportion."

Doctors thought they could cure diseases by bringing the body fluids into balance. They restored the balance in one of four ways. They changed the diet. They gave the patient a powerful laxative. They caused the patient to vomit. Or, they opened a vein and drained blood.

Medical schools still taught the methods of Galen and Hippocrates. Students learned medicine by looking up what Hippocrates or Galen said upon the subject. In fact, a student could earn a medical degree simply by reading these books and proving his mastery of them!

The sorry state of medical practice in England became a personal problem for Robyn. He nearly met his death from medicine given to him by mistake.

Soon after the Easter term opened, Robyn suffered a serious fever. He slowly recovered, but the bout with the illness weakened him. As a final treatment, Robyn's doctor prescribed what was supposed to be a refreshing tonic. Early in the morning the apothecary who mixed the medicine delivered it to Mr. Harrison's house where Robyn lived.

Unknown to Robyn and the doctor, the apothecary mixed the wrong medicine. Instead of a mild tonic, he sent Robyn a powerful emetic, a liquid to induce vomiting. The doctor had ordered the medicine for another patient to put that patient's humors in balance.

Cathy, the serving maid, brought the bottle to Robyn's room. She set the tonic on a table by the door. Two of Robyn's friends came to the room with her. Cathy stepped out of the room, leaving Robyn with his friends.

"We came to ask how you are doing," one of the boys said.

"We brought you a get-well present," the other boy said. He presented Robyn with some candy.

"I feel nearly well," Robyn told them. He sampled some of the candy.

After talking for a few minutes, the boys started to leave.

"I shouldn't have eaten the sweets before breakfast," Robyn said. "My stomach feels queasy."

"Take your medicine," one of the boys suggested. "Maybe it will help."

Robyn opened the bottle and drank the medicine. A moment later, his face turned red. He put his hands to his throat.

"Oh!" Robyn cried. "I feel as if I'm going to turn inside out." He threw up violently.

Robyn's friends called Cathy. She sent for the doctor, who arrived quickly. The doctor sniffed at the bottle. "It's the wrong medicine!"

Robyn expelled everything from his stomach. His face turned ashen and sweat covered his forehead.

The doctor could not hide his concern. "The effects of a large dose are too much for a young boy," the doctor admitted. He ordered towels soaked in cold water and helped Robyn to bed. Finally, Robyn's stomach settled down. He fell into an exhausted sleep.

Although Robyn recovered from that misadventure, his medical problems didn't end. He spent his fall break of 1637 in London. There he came down with another fever. Doctors in London could not cure him. When he returned to Eton, the doctor there prescribed a laxative.

Cathy accepted the medicine from the apothecary. She uncorked the bottle and drew back at the intense odor. She knew Robyn's delicate health and remembered his bout with the emetic. She decided this medicine would only make him worse. She emptied the bottle and secretly replaced the strong laxative with milder prune juice.

She knocked at Robyn's door and entered with the medicine. "Here is the prescription," she said. She watched as Robyn drank it.

He made a face as he drank the medicine. "This stuff is loathsome," Robyn said. "I've never tasted anything so awful."

Later, Cathy returned and asked about his health. "How do you feel?" she asked.

"Much better," he said. "The doctor's prescription completely restored me to good health."

The servant girl giggled. "Well, young Mr. Boyle, perhaps part of the credit goes to me."

"What do you mean?" Robyn asked.

"I poured out the doctor's prescription and replaced it with prune juice," she confessed.

"Prune juice? Then why did it taste so bad?" Robyn wondered. He concluded that his dislike of the medicine fooled his sense of taste. "I assumed it would taste bad, and so it did."

It amazed Robyn that the serving girl did as much to restore his health as had the doctor.

Robyn called upon the doctor. "I want to thank you for your services," he said, "and pay my account."

The doctor said, "You can credit your quick recovery to the excellence of the medicine, which I prepared myself."

Robyn found it difficult to conceal his smile.

These incidents shook Robyn's confidence in doctors who practiced medicine from the ancient books. From then on, Robyn avoided doctors whenever possible. He resolved never again to put his health completely in their hands. As he grew older, he taught himself enough about medicine to treat minor ailments. He developed his own cough syrups, compresses for bruises, and various concoctions of leaves as remedies for scurvy.

Occasionally, his trial-and-error methods improved his health. At other times his methods only made matters worse. Even so, Robyn probably did no more damage than he would have by turning himself over to the ignorant doctors of his day.

Robyn's interest in medicine led him to a greater study of the new science. He found few modern books in the school library. However, Sir Henry Wotton stocked his personal library with recent books on science.

Robyn asked for permission to read books from Sir Henry's private library. Sir Henry readily agreed.

"Where should I begin?" Robyn asked.

Thoughtfully, Sir Henry said, "Begin with books by Galileo and Kepler." He pulled out books from the shelves, naming them as he stacked them in Robyn's arms. "*The New Astronomy* by John Kepler, published in 1609. *The Starry Messenger* by Galileo, published in 1610."

Sir Henry selected another book, *On the Motion of the Blood*, by William Harvey, written in 1628. As you know, Galen teaches that the liver manufactures blood, that the heart pumps it throughout the body, never to return. William Harvey calculated that in one hour the heart pumps seven gallons of blood."

"Can the liver make that much blood in an hour?" Robyn asked.

"No, at least William Harvey doesn't think so," Sir Henry said. "Instead, he believes the body reuses the blood."

"Is this merely his opinion?" Robyn asked.

"No, William Harvey bases his ideas upon a series of simple experiments. He explains them in the book. In one experiment he tied closed an artery. The artery bulged on the side nearest the heart. Then he tied a vein. It bulged on the other side. The side nearest the heart drained empty. Blood flows *away* from the heart in the arteries and *toward* the heart in the veins."

"How does the blood get from arteries to veins?" Robyn asked.

Sir Henry said, "William Harvey admits that he has never been able to trace any connection between the two types of vessels. But both arteries and veins divide and subdivide into finer and finer vessels. He believes the connections do exist. They are merely too small to see.''

That night Robyn read by candlelight until his eyes began hurting from the strain. He said his evening prayers and climbed into his big four-post bed. He pulled the curtains around the bed.

Frank and three of his friends returned from their late night snack. They sat across the room around the fireplace, talking quietly.

Once again a disaster waited to happen. Robyn and Frank lived in a room in John Harrison's home. It was one of the original buildings at Eton and almost two hundred years old. The changing weather, hot and cold, rain and dry, had weakened the brick walls.

Sleep did not come to Robyn right away. He was content to lie in bed and listen to Frank and his friends talk. The old building creaked and groaned, but Robyn didn't think anything of it.

Without warning, the wall tumbled down. It carried the ceiling of the room above with it. Bed, chairs, books and furniture fell from the room above. Robyn's bed crashed to the floor. Brick dust billowed around him.

Robyn cried out in surprise. He pulled the bed covers over his head.

Broken brick and splintered wood tumbled down upon Frank. The chair in which he was sitting shattered from the impact.

In a moment help arrived to dig the boys out of the rubble. Frank came out with his shirt torn to shreds. Somehow, the boys survived with only minor injuries.

Although Robyn had been in the worst of it, he fared better than the other boys. The bed covers, which he threw over his head, served as a strainer.

It filtered out the brick dust. The other boys coughed for hours because of the dust they'd breathed.

The disaster at Mr. Harrison's house did start Robyn thinking. So many times unexpected events put his life in danger: the overturned carriage in Four Mile Waters, the mixed-up prescription, the building collapse. Danger came upon him without warning, but in every case he escaped.

He had supposed the rescues to be chance events at the time. Now he realized his escape could not be put down to chance or luck. No, the hand of God protected his life. He would be ungrateful and, blind to think otherwise. Robyn resolved to lead a life worthy of such abundant care.

Carew wrote letters to the Great Earl. He reported on the progress of Robyn and Frank. These glowing reports described Robyn and Frank as cheerful students. Carew wrote, "They say their prayers regularly and are equally polite to everybody."

Carew avoided alarming the Great Earl with stories of Robyn's misadventures. Instead, he went to great lengths to convince the Great Earl that Robyn and Frank should stay at Eton.

Mr. Perkins, a London tailor, visited Eton to size the boys for new clothes. Later, when he visited the Great Earl, he passed along the latest news about the boys. For the first time, the Great Earl learned about Robyn's medical trials and the building collapse.

The Great Earl became suspicious. Why hadn't Carew told the whole story? Robyn's father wrote to Sir Henry. He asked Sir Henry to investigate.

When Sir Henry inquired, he found that Carew had a reason to keep the Boyle boys at Eton. Carew had fallen in love. He'd been seeing young Marie, daughter of the school's baker.

The Great Earl became alarmed that he might lose his best servant to marriage. He decided to cool the romance between Carew and the baker's daughter. In the spring of 1638 he called Carew home.

The Great Earl wrote to his boys, "You'll be withdrawn later in the year to continue your education elsewhere."

Robyn learned that his days at Eton would end with the fall 1638 term. It did not surprise him. Nor did it disappoint him. Robyn no longer had the same enthusiasm for his studies. John Harrison, his favorite teacher, had been replaced by a new, rigid fellow.

Before Robyn left Eton, Sir Henry invited him to another evening meal. The special guest this time was John Milton, a thirty year old poet. John Milton lived at his father's house at Horton, near Eton.

John Milton planned to visit Europe over the next two years. Before being seated for the meal, he studied the painting of Venice.

"I plan to visit Venice later this year," John Milton said.

"Venice is my favorite city," Sir Henry said. "I served there for several exciting years as Ambassador. Once, the Duke of Tuscany learned of a plot to poison James VI of Scotland. He sent me on a secret mission to Edinburgh to warn James VI of the plot. Later, when James ascended to the throne of England, he appointed me his special ambassador. I received important assignments and the King would have given me even greater assignments except . . ."

"Except what?" Robyn asked.

John Milton quoted, "*An ambassador is an honest man sent to lie abroad for the good of his country.*"

"Who said that?" Robyn asked.

Sir Henry confessed, "I said it in jest, but it came back to haunt me. What country would welcome a man who is famous for such an indiscreet remark? The King could no longer use my services as an ambassador. It ruined my diplomatic career. Now I give better advice: '*Always tell the truth; for you will never be believed!*' "

With the end of the fall term in 1638, Robyn's stay at Eton ended. The Great Earl called his children together for Christmas. Robyn looked forward to a pleasant family reunion. However, before it was over, the Great Earl received terrible news from Ireland. The family gathering turned into a council of war.

# 4

# "Attend To Your Fortifications!"

Late in the fall of 1638, the five Boyle brothers rode together along the English countryside. Their destination was Stalbridge, the Great Earl's manor in England. The affairs of state took the Great Earl to England often. He bought Stalbridge so he could live there and more closely direct his dealings with Charles I, the English King. The manor was 60 miles south of Bristol in the rolling hills of Dorsetshire.

Robyn enjoyed the warm reunion with his four brothers. They rode along Dorsetshire lanes, which were bordered on each side by tangled hedges. The lanes took them through a country of thick woods broken by soft green pastures. A bird sang. A sheep dog barked. Grazing cattle raised their heads and watched through sleepy eyes as the horsemen passed.

Richard, Lord Dungarvan, was 26 years old. He'd been on a secret mission to see Charles I. An important decision came from that meeting, but Richard refused to give any details. He seemed barely able to contain his excitement.

Lewis, Viscount Kenelmeaky, was 19 years old. Roger, Baron Broghill, was 18 years old. Lewis and Roger had just finished studying for three years in Europe. Their French tutor took them on a grand tour of France, Holland and Switzerland. The two brothers still dressed in the style of foreigners. They even spoke with a bit of a French accent.

Monsieur Isaac Marcombes was the Frenchman who conducted Lewis and Roger on their foreign travels. Monsieur Marcombes rode ahead, allowing the Boyle brothers time to themselves.

Francis, called Frank, was almost 16 years old. He'd recently received the title of Lord Shannon.

Robert, called Robyn, was 12 years old. Robyn was tall for his age, but slender, and rather pale from spending too much time indoors. Robyn rode on a horse he'd purchased with his own money.

Robyn was stiff in the saddle as he approached Stalbridge. They'd ridden almost sixty miles in a single day. The manor stood among elm and chestnut trees. Hay fields, orchards and untouched forest surrounded Stalbridge.

They turned into the lane. Several yards ahead, a closed gate blocked their way. As they approached the gate, they heard a heated argument. Monsieur Marcombes, the French tutor, barely controlled his horse as it pranced back and forth in front of the locked gate. The Frenchman looked ready to charge ahead.

A man on the other side sat smug and self-assured on his horse. He held his head in the air, looking down at the Frenchman with distaste.

"Uh oh," Lewis said. "Monsieur Marcombes is angry."

Roger explained, "Although Monsieur Marcombes

is in every way a gentleman, he does have a temper. The person who makes him angry places himself in grave danger.''

"Here! What is this?'' Richard said. He kicked his horse into action. "Monsieur Marcombes is with us. Open the gate.''

The man at the gate stood his ground. "My name is Tom Murry. Lord Cork has placed *me* in charge of Stalbridge.''

Richard said, "I am Lord Dungarvan. I am the Great Earl's eldest son. These are my brothers: Viscount Kenelmeaky, Baron Broghill, Lord Shannon, and our youngest brother, Robert. The French gentleman is our guest.''

"Your father is not here,'' Tom Murry said. "I have no instructions regarding guests.'' The man's right hand lightly touched the handle of the pistol in his belt.

Richard spoke with cool confidence. "We will enter. You will accompany us and attend to the horses. Call the house staff together. They will prepare meals and ready our rooms. Any questions?''

For a moment Tom Murry tightened the grip on his horse's reigns. Then he dismounted, bowed stiffly and opened the gate. "Welcome to Stalbridge, Lord Dungarvan.''

As Robyn rode closer to the manor, he noticed signs of neglect. The orchards needed to be thinned, gates and fences repaired, new drains laid and thatching done. Loose brick had fallen from the chimney of the manor. Boards covered broken panes of glass. A patch covered a hole in the roof.

Richard surveyed the buildings and grounds. "Our father's house of Stalbridge. He has never seen the place.'' He added, "When he does, he'll make some changes!''

A few days later the Great Earl arrived. Robyn assumed he would dismiss Tom Murry, the property caretaker. Robyn spoke to his father about the matter. "He has proven himself to be incompetent to manage the estate."

The Great Earl said, "I shall give the man another chance. I purchased Stalbridge two years ago. During that time I have not made a single appearance here. Mr. Tom Murry managed without any direct orders from me. Once I explain exactly what I want, he'll be more successful."

The Great Earl personally drew up a long list of rules to help Tom Murry care for Stalbridge. The Great Earl called together the large household staff and addressed them. He personally instructed the clerk of the kitchen.

Immediately the Great Earl began to make over the buildings and grounds. He ordered leaden pipes to carry water. He purchased new furniture from London. He directed Tom Murry to pave paths and terraces in stone. He called in carpenters to rebuild the stairs. He hired stone masons to repair the chimney.

The Great Earl filled the larder with dried beef, cured bacon and salted salmon. Soon everyone knew the Great Earl was in charge.

The family gathered at Stalbridge for the Christmas holidays. Alice (Lady Barrimore), Lettice (Lady Goring), Catharine (Lady Ranelagh) and the little Lady Mary Boyle, all assembled at Stalbridge, together with several of the grandchildren.

Not everyone could be there. Smallpox struck Lady Dungarvan, Richard's wife. She postponed a visit to Stalbridge until she recovered. Dorothy, another daughter of the Great Earl, and her husband, Arthur Loftus, stayed in Ireland. Saddest of all, Lady Margaret Boyle, known as little Peggy, died in June

1637 at age eight years. She was the only child of the Great Earl younger than Robyn.

Robyn hugged Catharine, his favorite sister. She impressed him with her clever mind, charm and piety. Everyone agreed that she possessed the finest mind, the strongest character, the most beautiful face—and the most miserable marriage. Her husband, Arthur Jones impressed people, too, but in the other way. He gambled, played cards to all hours, and seldom came home sober.

The Great Earl selected who his children would marry. In the case of Arthur Jones, the Great Earl made a poor choice. After Arthur married Catharine, he carried her off to the gloomy Athlone Castle in the north of Ireland. There he abandoned her for months on end while he traveled to the larger cities for his drinking and gambling.

Despite her dismal marriage, Catharine retained her charm, shy good humor, and Christian piety. The visit to Stalbridge proved to be a great vacation for her. She radiated love, brightening a room when she entered it.

Everyone dressed in his or her finest clothes for the Christmas banquet. The Great Earl put on a waistcoat with a jerkin over it and over that a sleeveless and furred robe. He wore black velvet breeches. Like all prosperous men, he slung a gold chain across his chest and carried a rapier in his belt.

The Earl liked to give presents. Mr. Perkins, the London tailor, arrived with suits of scarlet and dublets of silver cloth for Frank and Robyn. The new clothes would be their Christmas gifts.

Lady Mary Boyle, the 15-year-old sister born between Frank and Robyn, was a talented horsewoman. The Great Earl gave her a saddle and saddlecloth of green velvet, laced and fringed with silver and green silk. He gave gifts of jewelry to his other daughters and daughters-in-law. He gave swords, pistols and dress clothing to his sons and sons-in-law. He gave small gowns of satin and scarlet to his grandchildren.

The children presented the Great Earl with laced shirts and nightcaps made for him with their own hands. People throughout the British Empire sent presents to the Great Earl. The simple gifts, made by the hands of his children, pleased the Great Earl the most. He kept the shirts and nightcaps. The other presents he passed on to his servants and to the poor people who worked for him.

The entire family enjoyed the warm fellowship of the Christmas season. Some people wondered how such a family could be so close. The Great Earl sent his sons to boarding schools or to live with governors. He sent his daughters to be raised in the homes of their future husbands. Yet, despite the far-flung family, the brothers and sisters held one another and their father in enormous respect and warm affection.

The next morning, Sunday, the Great Earl led his household to church. After the service, Catharine impressed everyone with her remarkable memory. After finishing the noonday meal, she retired to the study. There she took a quill pen and began writing.

"What are you writing?" Robyn asked.

"I'm writing the sermon that we heard this morning," Catharine explained.

"The minister preached for more than half an hour," Robyn said. He looked over her shoulder as she wrote the opening prayer, *Oh, ye Children of men, blesse ye the LORD. Praise him and magnifie him for ever.* Catharine penned the entire sermon word for word.

Robyn could only marvel at her memory.

After Christmas, the Great Earl called his sons

together. It was a cold morning but very pleasant where Robyn stood by the fireside. Split wood from an old cherry tree burned in the fireplace. It released a pleasant scent.

Robyn looked at his brothers one by one: Richard, Roger, Lewis and Frank. Present, too, was Alice's husband, Lord Barrimore, whom the Great Earl trusted as much as one of his own sons. The older boys, Richard especially, listened to their father with a grim and determined expression.

The Great Earl said, "The last two years have been trying times in Ireland. Affairs in Ireland have been troublesome. I've managed to acquire a number of enemies who resent my success. Chief among those enemies is Wentworth, whom Charles I appointed as Lord Deputy over Ireland. Lord Deputy Wentworth has hatched a scheme to charge me with crimes against the Crown."

"You've never done anything except support the King!" Robyn cried.

The Great Earl said, "Wentworth knows that the charges are all lies. He faked them to damage my reputation in Ireland and as a convenient way to raise money. If the courts find me guilty, they'll impose huge fines against me."

Lord Barrimore said, "His Majesty does need money. For several years he and Parliament have been engaged in a running quarrel. Parliament refuses to provide enough money to run the government. His Majesty has ordered his ministers to fill the treasury in whatever way they can."

"It's unfair!" Robyn said.

The Great Earl nodded. "If the King only knew how unfair the fines are, he would not accept a penny of them. For the last two years I've fought the matter in court. I fear it will drag on for years longer."

Richard, the Great Earl's oldest son, stood and faced his father. "Please don't be angry with me," Richard said, addressing his father. "I have met secretly with the King about this matter."

The Great Earl's face turned red. "This is a sensitive issue. Interference by outsiders will only make matters worse."

Richard stood his ground. "I am hardly an outsider."

The Great Earl grumbled. "Yes, of course. What did you propose to the King?"

Richard said, "King Charles faces a rebellion in Scotland . . ."

The Great Earl interrupted. "Events in Scotland are no concern of ours."

Robyn knew about the problem. Whoever ruled the land also ruled the religion of the country. Charles I controlled how his subjects worshiped. Under such circumstances, religious unrest often resulted. The King, as head of the Church of England, chose certain bishops to be over the church in Scotland. He insisted that the Scots accept the authority of his bishops. The Scots disagreed. They rebelled against the King.

Richard said, "The King desperately needs troops for the fight with Scotland. I offered to raise a hundred men and lead them into battle on the side of the crown."

The Great Earl jumped up. He began pacing, thinking about the plan. "Will the King drop the charges against my Irish estates?" he asked..

"Not entirely," Richard said. "He has agreed to settle the matter provided we pay 15,000 pounds into his treasury."

Robyn drew in his breath. *Fifteen thousand pounds*! It was an immense sum.

The Great Earl said, "I can't raise that much money."

Richard said, "His Majesty suggested you could pay in installments. I have no doubt that if you agree to it, your troubles in court will be over."

The Great Earl walked to the window. He stared outside, turning his back on those in the room. Robyn glanced from his father to Richard. He could feel the tension. Richard had taken an enormous risk in meeting with Charles I in secret. Never before had the Great Earl allowed anyone else to fight his battles. Would the Great Earl's pride prevent him from accepting Richard's plan?

The Great Earl turned. "Yes! You did well Richard. I will pay the fine. I'll outfit your horsemen for battle in Scotland, too."

Roger jumped up. "Lewis and I will fight at our brother's side," he said.

Over the next few weeks, the troop of one hundred

men assembled at Stalbridge. The Great Earl bought swords, pikes, helmets and light armor for them. With Richard in the lead, the line of horse soldiers rode off to join Charles I at Newcastle.

Frank and Robyn tried to volunteer, too. The Great Earl would hear none of it. "Three of my sons go into battle today. Three is enough. The world is never short of wars. You'll have the opportunity to prove yourself in battle when you are older."

The Great Earl turned to wave once again at the line of horsemen. Under his breath he prayed, "Restore them safe, happy, and victorious to me."

Robyn had heard a rumor that some of the English landlords faced rebellion from their Irish subjects. "Do you expect the Irish to rebel, too, like the Scots?"

The Great Earl said, "There will be no rebellion in Ireland. The Irish are too poor to equip an army."

Perhaps the Great Earl spoke with more confidence than he felt. Although he remained in England, he sent word to Ireland to have Lismore Castle and Youghal harbor strenghtened. To his property managers he sent the order, "Attend to your fortifications!"

# 5

# A Royal Wedding

Robyn and Frank stayed at Stalbridge while their older brothers were away in Scotland. During the day the boys went hunting, fishing and riding. At night they attended dinner parties and private theatrical plays.

After a few days of this, the Great Earl called the boys together. He told them, "There are too many distractions at Stalbridge for it to be a suitable place for young gentlemen."

He arranged for them to board with Mr. Dowch, a retired parson. The Great Earl explained, "Mr. Dowch is a person of excellent education. He will tutor you and supervise your activities."

Robyn objected. "I want to stay at Stalbridge so I can be with you."

The aging Great Earl enjoyed the company of his youngest sons. He could not bear the thought of sending them far from home. "Mr. Dowch lives in the village over the hill, less than two musket shots away. You will be close to Stalbridge and able to visit often."

Tests conducted by Mr. Dowch showed that Robyn's grasp of Latin had faded since the time at Eton. Mr. Dowch proceeded to drill Robyn in that classical language. The study bored Robyn. However, most scientists wrote in Latin, even the modern ones. Robyn endured the study, but only so he could read books not printed in any other language.

Mr. Dowch rewarded Robyn's intense study with days of freedom. Robyn could do as he wished, to read, or dream, or go exploring.

Robyn often left the village. He hiked across the fields and walked through the woods and along the river bank. After reading a book that sparked his imagination, he would become lost in thought. His imagination became a stage play, like the plays sometimes put on at Stalbridge. He acted out adventure stories, making himself the hero, of course. This day-dreaming was not just temporary. It stayed with Robyn all his life. At times he became ashamed that he spent so much time in thinking at random. He would bring himself back to reality by forcing himself to solve arithmetic problems in his head.

Robyn stayed with Mr. Dowch for only a short time. Frank became ill with a contagious disease. Rather than risk Robyn's health, the Great Earl called Robyn back to Stalbridge. There he put him under the charge of Monsieur Marcombes.

"I have complete confidence in Monsieur Marcombes," the Great Earl said. "When it came time to send Lewis and Roger to Europe, I asked Sir Henry Wotton to recommend a governor. He said that Monsieur Isaac Marcombes appeared to have been born for my purpose. Monsieur Marcombes served your brothers well. He can speak English, French and Italian. He's an ex-soldier, scholar and experienced traveler. He returned Lewis and Roger home healthy, mature, and with their Christian faith still strong.''

In appearance, dress and manner Monsieur Marcombes was very much a Frenchman. He had a skeptical mind. Monsieur Marcombes questioned what he read or heard. He taught Robyn to do likewise.

''I despise empty book learning,'' Monsieur Marcombes told Robyn. ''Put the books to the test of practical experience. Read critically. Think. Ask yourself, 'Does my experience agree with what I read?' ''

When he returned to his studies, Robyn sought out books on mines and metals. To his surprise, he found only one book, *About Metallurgy*, on the subject. Georgius Agricola, a German, wrote the book about 50 years earlier. The book summarized all the practical knowledge gained by miners since ancient Roman times. The book disappointed Robyn because it contained so few new facts.

Robyn asked Monsieur Marcombes, ''Surely advances have been made in mining during all these years?''

''Perhaps they have,'' Monsieur Marcombes said. ''However, people keep their discoveries secret in the hope of making a profit from them. Undoubtedly, the same discovery is made time and again, only to be lost when the person dies.''

Robyn soon learned how Monsieur Marcombes taught. When alone with Robyn, he corrected him, pointing out in no uncertain terms what he had done wrong. On the other hand, in the presence of others, Monsieur Marcombes always spoke highly of Robyn's good qualities. He avoided mention of any failings.

For instance, when the Great Earl asked about Robyn's progress, Monsieur Marcombes said, ''I've never met a person with such an insatiable curiosity about everything in heaven and earth. Your son has the finest mind I've ever had the privilege to develop.''

Such praise served to convince the Great Earl that he'd made the right choice in a tutor for his son. When Frank recovered from his illness, the Great Earl called him home. He put both Frank and Robyn under the care of the French tutor.

The Great Earl could see that Frank's interest in formal schooling had ebbed. The Great Earl ordered Monsieur Marcombes to begin planning to take Frank on an educational tour of Europe.

Monsieur Marcombes agreed, ''A visit to Europe is essential for the complete education of an English gentleman.''

Europe! France, Switzerland and Italy. Robyn remembered all the wonderful stories told by Sir Henry Wotton. ''I must go, too,'' Robyn told his father.

''Robyn is young,'' Monsieur Marcombes said, ''but he'll benefit from the trip as much as Frank.''

Thoughtfully, the Great Earl considered his son's request. Robyn was only twelve years old.

Robyn pressed ahead. ''I am not only Frank's brother, but his best friend, too. He'll enjoy the trip much more if I travel with him.''

''Very well,'' the Great Earl agreed. ''Make plans to take both of them.''

Before the boys left, the Great Earl searched for the right wife for Frank. ''She must be a girl from a prominent, well-to-do family,'' the Great Earl decided.

The name of Elizabeth Killigrew soon came to his attention. She was young, beautiful and the daughter of wealthy parents. Elizabeth, called Betty, was one of the Queen's maids-of-honor.

Sir Thomas Stafford, her step-father, served as

gentleman escort to the Queen. He introduced visitors and seated them according to their rank. Frank's marriage to Betty would certainly strengthen the Great Earl's standing in the court of Charles I.

Once Robyn heard of the marriage plans, he asked Frank for details.

Frank knew hardly more about the matter than Robyn. Frank said, "During all the discussions, neither our father nor Sir Thomas consulted me. I've not even seen Betty."

"I hear she is beautiful," Robyn said. "When will the marriage take place?"

Frank said, "Betty is only fourteen years old. Father is merely arranging the marriage contract now. The ceremony will not take place for two or three years, after we return from Europe."

Sir Thomas and Lady Stafford visited Stalbridge. The two families soon agreed on the terms of the marriage contract. Each family offered title to land and certain other royal privileges to Frank and Betty. This united not only the bride and groom, but their families as well.

On September 19, 1639, the Great Earl sent Frank to London to pay formal respects to his future bride. Monsieur Marcombes and Robyn went with him.

Robyn found London to be a confusing city, filled with many twisty, narrow lanes. Without Monsieur Marcombes to guide the way, he would have instantly become lost. Finally they turned onto the beautiful and broad Pall Mall. They walked along Pall Mall and turned onto Whitehall, which took them to the King's residence.

Charles met personally with Frank and Robyn. The King was shorter and less dignified than Robyn expected. Charles I seemed shy and greeted the boys courteously. To Robyn's amazement, the King spoke with a slight stammer.

Robyn expected to be in awe of the great King. Instead, he developed a real affection for the man. He thought of Charles as a favorite uncle rather than the ruler of the British Empire.

Although Charles I agreed to Frank's plans for foreign travel, he added, "A complete and perfect marriage at this time will be most convenient and honorable for all parties."

"What does that mean?" Frank whispered to Robyn.

Robyn said, "He wants you to marry little Betty *before* you go off to Europe."

Charles I had his way, of course. In October, the Great Earl of Cork and the rest of Frank's family set out from Stalbridge for the wedding in London.

On October 24, everyone assembled in the King's chapel. The event took place with all the pomp demanded by the marriage of a maid of honor to the son of the wealthy Great Earl of Cork. The King and Queen attended. Charles I himself gave away the bride.

A royal marriage feast followed the wedding. The family spared no expense to impress the great Lords and Ladies. Robyn sat next to his sister, Lady Mary Boyle. He nibbled at the asparagus souffle, which he didn't like. He wondered if he could ask for second helpings of pheasant and gingerbread. Those foods he did like.

"It is difficult for me to think of Frank as a married man," Robyn said.

Mary asked, "How difficult is it to think of yourself in the same condition?"

"Me? Married? What do you mean?" Robyn asked.

Lady Mary explained, "Father has already selected your bride. After you came to London, he rode out to Hatfield. He presented a gold and diamond ring to young Lady Ann, daughter of Lord Howard. Her family pledged that she shall become your wife."

Could his sister be teasing, Robyn wondered. No, she spoke in earnest.

Lady Mary Boyle continued, "He's selected my husband, too, most likely." With sudden intensity, she added, "I'll never consent to marriage, especially if the husband chosen for me is as bad as some of our brothers-in-law."

Robyn looked at her, aghast. Like his sister, he wanted nothing to do with marriage. Unlike her, he could not imagine going against his father's will. What could he possibly do?

As the marriage feast ended, Robyn's father stood

to make an announcement. For a heart-stopping moment, Robyn feared the Great Earl intended to proclaim Robyn's engagement to Lady Ann Howard. Instead, the Great Earl announced that Frank's marriage would delay but not cancel the plans for foreign travel. The Great Earl said, "Monsieur Marcombes, my son Robert and Lord Shannon will leave London on October 28."

Robyn enjoyed reading stories of foreign travel and adventure. Now he would go on a real adventure. He would learn firsthand about the world beyond Ireland and England. Robyn could hardly endure the suspense. During the next four days, he gingerly walked about, afraid something might come up to cause his father to cancel the trip.

Frank and Betty, of course, could hardly be pleased with the Great Earl's plans for them. The sixteen year old groom would go off to Europe. The fourteen year old bride would stay in London. What a honeymoon!

On October 28, Robyn dressed early in the morning and carried his bags outside. There he and Monsieur Marcombes loaded the horses for the ride to the harbor at Rye. A few minutes later the Great Earl joined them.

"We're ready to go," Robyn told his father, "except for Frank."

"Where is that boy!" the Great Earl demanded. "I sent for him an hour ago."

Monsieur Marcombes said, "Perhaps he is bidding good-bye to his bride. A honeymoon of only four days may be too brief for the young couple."

"He will see her again in one or two years," the Great Earl said. He turned to a servant. "Tell Lord Shannon that I demand his presence at once."

After a long delay, Frank finally appeared. Clothes hung out of his bag, which he had packed in haste.

Frank was terribly flustered. Suddenly he slapped his forehead. He turned to run back inside. "I dressed so quickly I forgot to buckle on my sword. I'll go back for it."

His father grabbed Frank's arm, restraining him. "You can buy another one during your travels. Mount up and move out."

Charles I appeared on the doorstep to offer his hand to the boys. He wished them a safe journey.

The little party rode to Rye in Sussex. There they hired passage on a ship. The seas in the English Channel proved rough, but the winds were favorable. They spent a day and a night at sea. They landed safely at Dieppe in France the next morning.

They traveled cross country from Dieppe to Rouen on the Seine. From there the party generally followed the banks of the river to Paris. They arrived in Paris on November 4.

Before their departure, the Great Earl gave the boys a case of pistols. In his haste to leave, Frank not only forgot his sword, but the case of pistols, too.

Monsieur Marcombes bought each of them a pair

of pistols, Highway robbers made travel dangerous, so travelers usually wore a sword and carried a brace of pistols in their belts.

For Frank, Monsieur Marcombes bought a bilboa, a short Spanish sword. Frank had received many wedding gifts of silk and satin clothes. He dressed in his best clothes and buckled on the sword. Frank turned around, letting Robyn see the complete outfit: sword, pistols and fancy trousers and shirt cut in the latest style. "How do I look?" Frank asked.

Robyn tried to keep the jealousy out of his voice. "Good enough, I suppose," he said.

"What's wrong?" Frank asked.

Monsieur Marcombes said, "I fear the green-eyed monster has raised its fearsome head."

"What do you mean?" Robyn asked.

"Envy is the green-eyed monster," Monsieur Marcombes explained.

Robyn tried to defend himself. "My sword is old and out of style. My clothes look too English for travel in Europe."

Monsieur Marcombes said, "Well, new sword and clothes make a small request." He bought Robyn a Spanish sword exactly like Frank's. He furnished Robyn with a complete black satin suit, the cloak lined with plush. The boys were ready to go.

The little band of travelers joined a group of twenty horsemen riding to Lyons. From Lyons they crossed the Alps to Geneva in Switzerland. That leg of the journey took three days. The entire trip from London to Geneva took almost a month.

"We will spend the winter in Geneva," Monsieur Marcombes said. "Next year, if your father agrees, we'll go on to Italy."

Robyn and Frank soon learned the reason Monsieur Marcombes wanted to settle for a while in

Geneva. His wife and family lived there. Monsieur Marcombes kept his wife and family a secret from the Great Earl. Perhaps he feared the Great Earl might think a family would distract Monsieur Marcombes from giving his full attention to Robyn and Frank.

Robyn and Frank lived in the Marcombes's home. They ate hearty meals. Every day Madame Marcombes cooked for them. She baked fresh bread and served dishes of fruit and Swiss cheese. Three days a week she roasted beef or mutton. On the other days she served fresh baked fish.

Geneva experienced a severe winter with large snowfall and cold weather. The boys slept snugly in the Marcombes home. A fire burned constantly in the fireplace in their bed chambers.

Their days in Geneva were not idle. Monsieur Marcombes set a schedule for them. Every morning, he taught them Latin grammar and logic. They read Roman history in French.

Robyn and Frank also studied the Bible from cover to cover. In the morning they read two chapters from the Old Testament. In the evening they read two chapters from the New Testament. Monsieur Marcombes discussed the Scriptures with them. As a Bible scholar he could help them with the passages they didn't understand. They attended church twice a week. They said their prayers morning and evening.

For exercise, the boys took lessons from a fencing master. Frank took up gymnastics. He learned to vault and tumble. Robyn played paddle tennis. This sport remained a favorite with him throughout his younger days. Of course, he would rather read an interesting book any day.

After dinner they studied geometry, geography, astronomy and fortification.

"Fortification is a branch of geometry," Monsieur

Marcombes explained. "Geometry helps you construct a fortress and defend it against assault. You must calculate angles for fields of fire and learn the proper placement of cannons. Here is a drawing of a fortified castle as it would appear from overhead—a bird's-eye view."

Robyn examined the drawing. It showed the castle at the center of a beautiful and precise figure, like a starfish. Despite his dreamy nature, and a tendency to read adventure stories, Robyn found geometry to be one of his better subjects.

"Every young English nobleman must learn fortification," Monsieur Marcombes explained, "particularly if you expect to inherit land in Ireland. Estates there must be strengthened and defended in case of an uprising by the Irish peasants."

"Father says the Irish will not rebel," Robyn objected.

Monsieur Marcombes said, "If all of the English landlords treated their subjects as well as your father, there would be no cause for alarm. However, some of the provinces in northern Ireland are perilously close to an uprising."

"Where would they find money to outfit an army?" Robyn asked.

Monsieur Marcombes said, "England has many enemies. These enemies will help Ireland simply to complicate matters for England."

Rumors of strife in Ireland continued to surface. In February, 1640, Robyn received the first letters from home. To his relief, the Great Earl mentioned nothing of rebellion in Ireland.

Spring came to Geneva. Monsieur Marcombes hired horses for a three week vacation into the mountains. The boys stayed at a chateau, a hotel in the style of a French manor, high in the Alps.

That night the air became still. Even after midnight, the air remained hot and oppressive. A sudden loud clap of thunder awakened Robyn from a sound sleep. A violent storm broke the charged atmosphere. Robyn rushed to the window. Strong winds blew through the mountain pass. Dazzling lightning froze the landscape in stark white.

The roar of the wind drowned the noise of the thunder. The rains almost swallowed the flashes of lightning.

Robyn had never experienced such a frightening storm. He concluded that the Day of Judgment must be at hand. The storm filled Robyn with a sudden realization that he wasn't prepared to stand before the throne of judgment. He trembled as the winds and thunder shook the chateau.

Robyn prayed for God to preserve him from the storm. He promised that if he survived the storm, he would live a Christian life.

The morning broke clear and cloudless. Robyn felt ashamed that it took a storm to turn his mind to Jesus. Then he remembered the apostles who sailed across Lake Galilee. A storm struck their fishing boat. They feared for their lives, thinking they would sink. Then the apostles remembered that Jesus was asleep in the back of the boat. They woke Him, and when they did, He calmed the storm.

Robyn had let Jesus go to sleep in the back of his mind, even as the apostles let Jesus go to sleep in the back of their boat. A storm made the apostles realize they needed Jesus. A storm made Robyn realize that he needed Jesus, too.

"To inherit a good religion is not enough," Robyn decided. He sought a personal faith, one based squarely on the Bible. Robyn plunged into a study of Scripture. He began to teach himself Hebrew, Aramaic and Syriac. These languages, together with Latin and Greek, enabled him to read the ancient biblical texts.

At that time Geneva enjoyed an unusually tolerant religious atmosphere. Many prominent Christian leaders lived in the independent city. They felt free to debate religious matters with one another. Robyn found the discussions exciting.

Summer passed.

Frank's thoughts turned to his bride. "Our trip to Europe will end when we finish with Italy. The sooner we go there, the sooner I can return home to Betty.''

Robyn wanted to see Italy, too. He hoped to meet Galileo, the world's best known scientist. The aged Galileo still lived in Italy, in a small town outside Florence.

Together, Robyn and Frank urged Monsieur Marcombes to ask their father for permission to take them to Italy.

Mail arrived from England. The Great Earl refused to give his permission. Monsieur Marcombes explained, ''The English and Italians are not on the best of terms with one another. A mob in London murdered a Catholic priest from Italy. Your father fears Italy will be unsafe for English visitors.''

''What can we do?'' Robyn asked.

''I'll think of something,'' Monsieur Marcombes promised.

# 6

# The Desperate Journey

Robyn and Frank lived in Geneva with Marcombes and his family not only through the winter of 1639, but also the winter of 1640 as well. The Great Earl *still* refused to give permission for the trip to Italy. "Italy is not safe for English visitors," the Great Earl wrote.

After sixteen months, the boys became restless. "We must do something to change our father's mind," Robyn said. "Otherwise, we'll never see Italy."

Robyn wrote to his father. "My most honored Lord and father, I desire with passion and without any question to go into Italy. The trip will help us learn the language. We will learn about astronomy and architecture and see many remarkable sights."

Monsieur Marcombes developed a plan. He wrote to the Great Earl, "Since Englishmen aren't safe in Italy, we'll travel as visitors from France. All and always, the boys will speak in French. They have become perfect in that tongue and can visit Italy and pass as Frenchmen.''

He promised to be constantly on the watch for their safety. He pointed out that he'd already been prepared to shoot his way through robbers who might have ambushed them on the way from France. '' I will keep the boys safe,'' he assured the Great Earl.

In addition, Monsieur Marcombes insisted upon a letter from Charles I. ''The letter, written in Latin, should mention me by name. King Charles should ask all kings, princes and magistrates to give us whatever protection we might need during our travels.''

After a long delay, the Great Earl wrote back. He'd moved from Stalbridge to Ireland. He lived at Castle Lyons, the home of his eldest daughter Alice and her husband Lord Barrimore.

The boys gathered around their governor to read the mail.

The Great Earl gave his approval.

The news overjoyed Robyn. The stammer, which he'd almost conquered, came back with full force. For some minutes he stammered so badly that Frank and Monsieur Marcombes could scarcely understand him. They turned away to keep from laughing.

As requested, the Great Earl supplied Marcombes with a letter of safe passage from Charles I. The Great Earl reminded Marcombes to take care of Robyn and Frank. ''I am entrusting my jewels to you in a strange country,'' the Great Earl wrote.

Monsieur Marcombes began immediate preparations for the Italian journey. He bought the boys three complete traveling suits. Madame Marcombes sewed new clothing for them, too.

''You'll dress in French or Italian fashion,''

Monsieur Marcombes said. "Speak Italian or French, but never English, even when you think you are alone."

In the fall of 1641, the trio set out for the long delayed trip to Italy.

The Rhine, an important river in Europe, tumbled down from the high Alps. There it began from melting snow. The party of travelers followed the river upstream. It became nothing but a tiny stream. Robyn stood with one foot on either side. The mighty river flowed as a brook between his legs.

They followed the river upstream to its headwaters in the distant mountains.

"Look at those peaks," Frank said. He gazed awe-struck at the snow-covered Alps.

Monsieur Marcombes said, "There's an enormous glacier there with solid ice thousands of feet thick. It has cracks in it hundreds of feet deep into which a man could fall and never be seen again."

Robyn and Frank, accomplished horsemen by now, rode into the high mountain passes.

Robyn looked at the clouds. They were white, just like clouds ought to be. They were fluffy as they hung in the sky, but with one difference. Robyn, Frank and Monsieur Marcombes rode along the mountain ridge *above* the clouds. The clouds spread out below them, filling a deep green valley.

From here Robyn could see that the people in the valley experienced an overcast sky and rainstorms. On top of the mountain, the little party of travelers enjoyed bright sunlight. Amazing!

At another spot they crossed over a great swatch of barren land. Monsieur Marcombes explained, "Twenty-five years ago an earthquake started a land-slide. It entirely covered the town of Piur."

"How deep did it bury the town?" Robyn asked.

"No one knows," Monsieur Marcombes said. "All attempts to dig down to it have failed."

They passed through cities Robyn had only read about before: Verona with an ancient amphitheater almost as large as the Colosseum in Rome; Padua where Galileo once taught; Venice where Marco Polo set off on his trips to China; finally Florence, the city of flowers, the most beautiful city in Italy.

Monsieur Marcombes sold the horses. He rented rooms in a boarding house. The boys settled down to pass the winter in Florence. Other travelers stayed there, including some Jewish Rabbis. Robyn enjoyed talking late into the night with them about Jewish customs. Robyn learned a great deal about the Law and Prophets—the Old Testament—from Jewish teachers.

Monsieur Marcombes conducted the boys from one sight to another. They visited the great cathedral of Florence. "The dome measures almost 140 feet across," Monsieur Marcombes said, "making it one of the largest in the world."

Robyn learned Italian well enough to speak and read it. The Great Earl sent the boys a generous allowance of 1000 pounds each year. Frank spent some of his allowance at the carnivals and jousting matches. Robyn used part of his allowance to buy books. He read everything in sight: Greek myths, Roman legends, Italian history, lives of great people, Bible studies and much more.

After visiting the bookseller, Robyn walked home carrying a book under each arm while reading a third one. This didn't make it particularly hard for him to walk. He never saw anything until Monsieur Marcombes or Frank tapped him on the shoulder to point out a sight. Here and there he peeked over the top of the book as he crossed the street.

Robyn spent many of his spare hours reading the works of Galileo. He read Galileo's *Dialogue on the Two Chief World Systems*. In it, Galileo presented evidence that the sun is the center of the planetary system. He argued that the earth is a planet like Mars and Venus. The more Robyn read, the more he admired the great Italian scientist.

When Galileo turned his telescope to the moon he found craters, mountains and valleys. "The surface of the moon is not perfectly smooth," he reported. "It is full of irregularities, uneven, full of hollows, much like the surface of the earth itself."

Aristotle had written that the heavens were perfect,

the moon a smooth ball, the sun an umblemished globe. Galileo examined the sun and found spots on it.

One professor said, "These things cannot be in the sky. Aristotle tells nothing of them. They must be the fault of Galileo's glass."

"Why do you blindly accept the writings of the ancients," Galileo cried. "Who can assure us that everything that can be known in the world is known already? Who can set bounds to man's understanding?"

Galileo urged scientists to take up the new science. "Avoid observations influenced by emotion, surmise or personal prejudice. Find the answer by conducting the proper experiment. Learn to measure, to weigh and to use mathematics."

Most professors still ignored Galileo's ideas.

Robyn learned that for several years the great stargazer had been blind, perhaps from looking at the sun through a telescope. A group of Galileo's enemies visited the astronomer. They mocked him for losing his sight. Galileo replied, "I had the satisfaction to see in heaven what no mortal eyes had ever seen there before."

Galileo lived in Arcetri, a small town near Florence. Monsieur Marcombes's letter from Charles I would have admitted Robyn to an audience before the great scientist. However, Galileo died during the winter on January 8, 1641.

"What will happen to science now that Galileo is gone?" Robyn wondered. "Who will replace him?"

Monsieur Marcombes said, "What Galileo started cannot die away. His ideas will endure. Some young person of imagination and dedication will take his place. Perhaps it will be you."

Robyn smiled at such an idea, but the suggestion did start him thinking. Because of his father's wealth,

Robyn could become a scientist. He could return to England and attend the best university, either Cambridge or Oxford. Unlike others who struggled to earn a living, Robyn could devote his full time to science if he wished. His father would buy equipment to outfit a laboratory. He could conduct whatever experiments interested him.

Robyn decided, "When I return to England, I'll become a scientist."

Toward the end of March, 1642, the visitors began their journey to Rome. After five days they safely arrived at that city.

"Rome," Robyn said under breath.

"The city served as the capital of Imperial Rome," Monsieur Marcombes said. "It is still one of the most important cities in the world."

Many of the magnificent Roman buildings still stood. The Forum and the Colosseum in the heart of ancient Rome impressed Robyn the most. The modern structures interested him the least.

By this time Robyn had learned to speak French fluently, almost as well as Monsieur Marcombes. His masquerade as a Frenchman proved completely successful. The little party moved about freely. So certain were they of their safety, they even entered the chapel of the Vatican. There they observed the pomp and splendor of the cardinals and the Pope.

What Robyn remembered best occurred after the service ended. A man put his handkerchief to the floor and swept into it the dust from the aisle where the Pope had walked.

One day in the middle of May, they walked outside the city to examine an aqueduct. "The Romans built the aqueducts to carry water to Rome. Once inside the city, the water is distributed through lead pipes."

Frank sat down in the shade of the arched waterway. "I've seen enough sights, either ancient or modern," he said.

Monsieur Marcombes spoke privately to Robyn. "Your brother is anxious to start home."

Robyn admitted that he'd seen enough in Rome, too. Then he added, "Betty wrote to Frank. She begged him to come back to her. She even threatened to come to him. Frank is growing more desperate. He fears she will leave him if this trip keeps him away much longer."

Thoughtfully, Monsieur Marcombes said, "We will start back. In the meantime, I'll keep a close watch on Frank, lest he decide to set out on his own."

They returned to Florence and then traveled down the Arno river to Pisa and on to Leghorn on the Mediterranean. There they purchased a felucca, a narrow, swift sailing vessel.

Monsieur Marcombes told Robyn, "I'll act as captain and you and Frank will be the crew."

"We've never sailed a ship before," Robyn pointed out.

"I'll instruct you in the basics of sailing. You can learn it in a day. We'll not venture too far out to sea. We'll draw our boat ashore at night or when a storm threatens."

"What is our route?" Robyn asked.

Monsieur unrolled a chart and traced out their route. "We'll touch land at Genoa, Monaco, Nice and Antibes. There we'll sell the ship and travel overland to Marseilles. Letters from your father should be waiting for us in Marseilles. He's sending the money for the final part of our journey."

The sea voyage turned out to be a carefree way to travel. Monsieur Marcombes kept the watch. Frank manned the tiller. Robyn set the sail. Once Robyn

trimmed the sails to Monsieur Marcombes's satisfaction, he could lie about and read. With the green sea below him, the blue sky above him, and a cool breeze blowing across him, Robyn could not have been more content.

While Robyn and Frank enjoyed their European vacation, events took a disastrous turn for their father in Ireland. Lord Barrimore threw a banquet for the Great Earl. Suddenly a messenger ran breathlessly into the banquet hall. He interrupted the festivities with an urgent message for the Great Earl.

"It's war!" the messenger told the Great Earl.

"The Irish have risen in a bloody outbreak against the English in Munster."

The revolt spread across Ireland. The Irish launched a furious assault on the English estates. The landowners retreated to their castles to take their stand.

Quickly, the Great Earl organized the resistance. "Lord Barrimore will strengthen Castle Lyons. Viscount Kenelmeaky will defend his mansion at Bandonbridge. Baron Broghill will hold Lismore."

The Great Earl retreated to Youghal to hold the vital harbor for supplies from England. He looked to Charles I for help. The help never came. Instead, the Great Earl had to pay for the entire battle out of his own pocket.

Only a few months earlier he'd been one of the most prosperous men in the English realm. Now he dedicated his fortune to raising arms for use in Ireland: kegs of powder, muskets, shot, pikes. The women stayed as long as they dared, then they fled to London. A few hundred English landlords and their private army stood against 200,000 armed Irishmen.

While Robyn and Frank enjoyed the pleasant Mediterranean sun, their father threw the last of his resources into the battle. No longer did he fight to preserve his lands, or even his wealth. If the Irish over ran the strongholds, they would put the Great Earl and his sons to the sword. The Great Earl fought desperately for sheer survival.

Robyn and Frank knew nothing of the terrible events in Ireland. Late in May, 1642, they arrived in Marseilles, where they expected to find letters from the Great Earl.

"Your father will send bills of exchange to carry us on to Paris and to Ireland," Monsieur Marcombes explained.

Without a trustworthy mail service, travelers delivered letters and parcels. Wealthy merchants often acted as banks, providing funds to travelers. The merchants balanced the books by sending one another letters of exchange. The Great Earl would pay Mr. Perkins, the London tailor. The tailor, in turn, would authorize merchants in Europe to advance money to Monsieur Marcombes. Later, when agents of Mr. Perkins came to Europe on business, they would repay the merchants.

In Marseilles, Mr. Castell, a traveling agent for Mr. Perkins, delivered the letter from the Great Earl.

Monsieur Marcombes opened the letter. The Great Earl had written the letter about two months earlier. The boys gathered around to hear the latest news from home.

"This is odd," Monsieur Marcombes said. He turned the envelope inside out. "There is a long letter from your father but no bills of exchange."

Monsieur Marcombes began reading the sad story of the fighting in Ireland. "Necessity compels me," the Great Earl wrote, "to make you know the dangerous and poor estate whereunto I am at this instant reduced." The letter went on to describe the difficulty the Great Earl faced to raise enough money to bring his boys home.

Monsieur Marcombes said, "Your father sold the household silver and raised 250 pounds. He made it over for Mr. Perkins to pay. He can spare no more because he needs every pound for the defense of Ireland."

The letter continued, "For with inward grief of soul I write this truth unto you that I am no longer able to supply them beyond this last payment. But if they serve God and be careful and discreet in their carriage, God will bless and provide for them as hitherto He has done for me."

The Great Earl advised, "My two young sons that are so dear to me should employ the 250 pounds to bring them home again."

Monsieur Marcombes said, "Your father wants you to join him at Youghal. If that harbor is closed, you should sail to Dublin."

"We must start for home at once," Frank said.

Monsieur Marcombes paged through the letter again. "There are no bills of exchange with this letter. Mr. Perkins must have kept the money for himself."

Robyn and Frank looked blankly at one another. "No money?" Robyn asked. He found it difficult to even understand what it meant to be without money.

They waited fruitlessly for the bills of exchange. During this time, they depended upon Monsieur Marcombes's limited funds for food and lodging. The money never did come.

After several days, Monsieur Marcombes said, "You must face the fact that you are eight hundred miles from Ireland and out of money. The cost of sending you home is too much for me."

"What are we going to do?" Robyn asked anxiously.

Frank said, "By some means or another I shall reach Ireland to stand by my father's side."

"I shall go, too," Robyn said.

During the days of indecision in Marseilles, Robyn became ill. A feverish light burned in his eyes. Even a short walk left him weak and breathless.

Monsieur Marcombes managed to secure a small loan from an agent of Mr. Diodato Diodati, a Geneva banker.

"There is not enough money for both of you," Monsieur Marcombes told the boys. "Frank, you shall make your way home as best you can. Robyn, you shall return to Geneva with me."

Robyn objected. Although he had no liking for war, family loyalty demanded that he return to Ireland. "I must fight with my father and brothers," Robyn said.

Monsieur Marcombes said gently, "A tired, ailing fifteen-year-old boy would be of slight help to the Great Earl. The sensible course is for you to go back to Geneva with me."

Frank did leave for Ireland. He managed to reach his father safely.

Robyn sent a letter to his father by way of Frank. The Great Earl's seventh son apologized for not being on the scene. "Although I cannot be there," Robyn wrote, "I will always strive to show myself to be an obedient son."

Frank arrived in time to take part in the battle of Liscarrol. All of the Earl's sons except Robyn fought in the battle. During the battle, a musket shot struck Lewis. He fell from his horse. The Great Earl's troops began to break rank and retreat.

Frank charged into the enemy. He rescued his unconscious brother. This decisive action rallied the men, and they repelled the enemy. However, Lewis didn't survive the battle. He died of the musket shot to his head. Lord Barrimore, the Great Earl's most faithful son-in-law, died in the fighting, too.

By July of 1643, the Irish launched an assault upon Lismore. The Great Earl's fortification held the first charge. The furious Irish withdrew and amassed for another charge. They planned to wear the defenders down. Eventually Lismore castle would fall into their hands.

The Great Earl never considered surrendering to the rebels.

Charles I took matters out of the Great Earl's hands.

Charles I decided to sign a peace treaty with the rebels. The treaty took the form of a surrender to the Irish. Charles I sacrificed the Great Earl's land to restore peace to Ireland.

Brokenhearted, the Great Earl went to bed and turned his face to the wall. He had lost so much: Barrimore and Lewis dead, his family scattered, his foundries ruined, his money spent, his possessions lost, his estates in the hands of others.

The Great Earl died as the truce was signed at Sigginstown in September, 1643.

For two fruitless years, Robyn lived in Geneva with his tutor. He learned of the disaster in Ireland and of the death of his father. Robyn had been keeping a journal of his travels. He stopped writing in his journal.

"I can no longer accept your charity," Robyn told his teacher. "I must go home."

Monsieur Marcombes purchased a string of jewels at a reasonable price. He gave the jewels to Robyn. "You can sell the gems to raise money during your journey," Monsieur Marcombes said.

"I shall repay you," Robyn promised. He clasped hands with his tutor. Then he abandoned his reserve and threw his arms around Monsieur Marcombes. They hugged in a final farewell.

Robyn set out on his own. He sold the gems one by one to pay his expenses. He rode across France. He sailed to England and at last reached London.

Robyn had begun his travels from this city. When he left he'd enjoyed every possible advantage. His future seemed secure. He could look forward to wealth, an estate in the country, and perhaps starting a family with Lady Ann Howard as his wife.

Now, five years later, Robyn walked the streets of London penniless and alone.

# 7

# The Invisible College

In the summer of 1644, the slim and suntanned Robert Boyle walked along the streets of London. During his five years abroad, he'd taken up European dress and speech. English citizens looked upon him as if he were a foreigner. He felt like a stranger in the city.

"Trust God," Robyn said to himself. "Do not worry. Pray for God's guidance. He will see you through."

Monsieur Marcombes had provided him with a letter of introduction. "The letter is to Dr. Theodore Diodati, a London physician," Monsieur Marcombes explained. "He is the brother of our banker friend in Geneva. Dr. Theodore Diodati lives in the parish of St. Bartholomew. He will put you in touch with the rest of your family."

England seethed with unrest. The Crown's problems with Parliament erupted into open warfare. Royal troops under Charles I battled Puritan troops led by Oliver Cromwell and Parliament. With

England divided and its strength weakened, fresh uprising broke out in Ireland and Scotland.

Robyn started to cross the street. He jumped back as a troop of soldiers swept by. Their swords rattled as their horses trotted along the dusty street.

Robyn felt utterly lost in the confusing jumble of streets. He despaired of ever finding his way to the doctor's home. As he neared St. Bartholomew, he walked along Aldersgate Street. A man and woman walked toward him. They talked earnestly to one another. The pair hardly noticed the activity around them.

Robyn stopped as they drew closer. He looked more closely at the woman. He blinked: once, twice, a third time. He could hardly believe his eyes.

"Catharine!" Robyn cried.

She looked him over carefully. "Robyn?" she asked, unsure of herself. "Is it really you?"

"Yes!" Robyn said.

Robyn hugged his sister. Tears of joy brimmed in his eyes. "I'm home at last," Robyn said. He couldn't contain his pleasure at seeing a familiar face.

Catharine stepped back and looked at him. "Why, you have grown up. I must remember to call you Robert rather than Robyn," she said. "You're too old to carry a child's nickname."

The man waited patiently as Robyn—Robert—and Catharine talked at the same time. Finally, Catharine said, "Robert, this is my friend John Milton."

Robert recognized the man. "Oh, yes, John Milton, the poet. I enjoyed the pleasure of your company at a dinner held by Sir Henry Wotton at Eton."

Catharine said, "Mr. Milton is headmaster of a private school. He also writes pamphlets in support of Parliament's position."

"Oh," Robert said lamely. He assumed his family would be on the side of Charles I and the Royalist upper classes. Robert asked, "Surely we support King Charles?"

Catharine said, "The matter is not as simple as it first appears. King Charles has meddled in religious affairs. His supporters, the Cavaliers, have lost the approval of good Puritan middle classes."

Robert knew that Cavaliers had a reputation for swearing, drinking, smoking, and living immoral lives.

John Milton said, "Your brother Roger began in the service of King Charles. However, at your sister's urging he has thrown his support behind Parliament. He agreed to help put down rebellions in Scotland or Ireland. Of, course, Cromwell is wise enough not to ask him to fight his fellow Royalists in England."

Catharine said, "London is in the hands of Parliament. The King and his Court have abandoned the city. They have fled to Oxford. The Queen has sailed to the Netherlands to raise money for her husband by selling the crown jewels.''

Robert put the matter aside. ''I have no mind for politics,'' he admitted. ''My head is full of philosophy and theology. But my purse is empty. I have no home.''

''You must stay with me,'' Catharine said. ''I'm living at St. James now. Later this year I'll move to a more spacious house at Pall Mall.''

Robert agreed. He could hardly do otherwise.

Catharine lived at St. James with her four children. After Catharine's husband wasted his fortune in gambling and drinking, he'd abandoned her. She received a little income from other members of the Boyle family and from the small remaining share of her father's wealth.

The loss of the Boyle fortune presented Robert with a painful duty. He would have to meet with Lady Ann and ask her to release him from the marriage contract. He dreaded the meeting. ''How will I tell her that I cannot support a family?'' he asked his sister.

''It isn't necessary,'' Catharine informed him. ''Once your fortune vanished, her father looked around for a more suitable groom. He decided she should marry Charles Howard, one of Cromwell's men.''

Relieved, Robert wrote to Monsieur Marcombes to report his safe arrival. ''I'm staying with my sister, Lady Ranelagh, in London. I found her by accident. For such an accident I give thankfulness to the providence of God. Although her estate is low, her house is the meeting place for England's best minds. She is a trusted friend of the chief thinkers of London.''

Catharine opened her house to the leading politicians, physicians, and philosophers of the day. They exchanged the latest news, whether political or scientific. Robert listened with keen interest to their discussions. Soon the scholarly guests noticed Robert's intelligence and invited him to join in the conversation.

He met and talked every day with prominent doctors, chemists, astronomers, mathematicians and religious leaders. They talked about the nature of comets, sun spots and shooting stars. They exchanged ideas ranging from the transfusion of blood to the smelting of metals from their ores. They studied the weather, musical instruments, and other topics of the new learning.

Poverty prevented Robert from receiving a university education. These informal meetings became the only college he ever attended.

"I call the group the *invisible college*," he wrote Monsieur Marcombes. "It serves me better than any real college."

Robert closed the letter by assuring Monsieur Marcombes that he would settle his account. "I shall pay you at the first opportunity," Robert promised.

"How can I raise the money?" Robert wondered aloud.

"Stalbridge," Catharine said. "The Great Earl wanted you to have it. He left it to you in his will."

"I must return to Stalbridge," Robert said. "It is the only way to manage the estate." He fondly remembered the happy times there, eating fruit from the orchards and walking at random while lost in thought.

Catharine warned him against expecting too much. "The main manor had been abandoned since your father died. Roads to it have been cut off by roving bands of armed men."

"Nevertheless I must go there and make the estate profitable," Robert decided.

"Traveling alone is too dangerous," Catharine
said. She insisted that Roger, Lord Broghill, accompany Robert to the property. As an extra measure,
she asked for the protection of Parliament. "I'll put
in a good word for you with my friends in the House
of Commons. They'll grant you permission to travel."

After spending five months with his sister, Robert
Boyle set out for Stalbridge in March 1646. Robert
was still a teenager. Roger rode with him.

Outside of Farnham the two Boyle brothers met a
traveler who reported disturbing news. "Cavaliers hold
the road ahead," the man said. "They're stopping
travelers and plundering any valuables."

Robert and Roger succeeded in reaching Farnham
safely. They ate supper and went to bed. Robert slept
in his clothes, a habit he always followed when traveling. He put his bilboa, the short Spanish sword, under
his pillow.

In the dead of night a loud and impatient knock
sounded at the door.

"Light a candle!" Robert urgently whispered to
his brother. Robert drew his sword from under his

pillow. He leaped out of the bed. He held the sword in one hand and pulled a pistol from the holster hanging on the bed post.

Roger drew his sword, too. He lit the candle. The thundering at the door continued.

Cautiously, Robert unbolted the door.

Soldiers burst into the room. They held their muskets level and ready. One of the men peered closely first at Roger and then at Robert. "These are not the men we look for," he said. The armed men whirled around and stormed off to search elsewhere.

The next morning Robert continued the journey. Along the Salisbury plain, near the mysterious Stonehenge ruins, a party of armed men surrounded them. They searched the baggage but let them pass. Several times armed bands from one side or the other stopped him. Robert took care not to offend either side.

Robert became more determined to stay out of the conflict. He regarded the English Civil War as barbaric and stupid. Robert cried to his brother, "What reasonable creatures, that call themselves Christians, too, should delight in such an unnatural thing as war?"

After passing through the most dangerous territory, Roger turned back, leaving Robert to go alone. That evening, a Saturday, Robert neared Stalbridge. The weather changed for the worse. Dark, grey clouds rolled across the sky. A steady, cold rain fell.

Robert nearly cried when he saw the condition of his country manor. Weeds overgrew the fields. The orchard needed trimming. The main manor house lay empty and in ruins. The cottages required extensive repairs.

"My own ruined cottage in the country!" Robert said. His voice choked with emotion.

Tom Murry, the caretaker, offered lame excuses for the dilapidated condition of the farm. Once again he'd let it become run-down.

"The Great Earl gave you a second chance," Robert said. "You must have known he would deal more harshly with you if you failed him again."

"Your father is dead," Tom Murry pointed out. Quickly, he added, "Sorry sir."

Robert said, "My late father willed the estate to me. I will act in his stead. You have proven yourself to be an unprofitable steward. Stalbridge no longer needs your services. I will manage Stalbridge myself."

"You? Hah! A gentleman farmer knows only how to attend dinner parties and go shooting. You will fail miserably," Tom Murry predicted. "Then you'll beg me to come back and put the farm in order."

Robert, like his father, did have a good head for business. He raised money quickly by cutting down some of the finer trees and selling them for lumber. With that money, he repaired buildings, dressed the orchards, planted crops and bought cattle. He restored the tenant cottages and attracted experienced farmers to the land. He collected rents from the tenant farmers.

Tom Murry came back to the farm. The man held his hat in his hand. He bowed his head and asked for mercy. "I've not been able to find steady employment elsewhere. Please, Mr. Boyle, take me back and I'll prove myself to you."

The kind-hearted Robert Boyle rehired the man. But he took the precaution of not putting Tom Murry in a position of trust.

Robert wrote Monsieur Marcombes and asked for help. "What I need now are practical books on farming. I need proven methods to grow good crops and raise healthy livestock."

Monsieur Marcombes promised to look for the

books and mail them to Robert. "I'll leave a standing order with the booksellers," Monsieur Marcombes wrote.

In the fall of 1646, Robert counted his money. The very first year, the estate showed a profit. It had been a grueling year. He missed his sister. He missed the activity in London. Most of all he missed the invisible college. Robert resolved to visit London more often.

In addition, he decided to build a laboratory at Stalbridge. There he would experiment with chemistry. Robert ordered tools for working with chemicals: crucibles, retorts, mortars, and various glassware for filtering, condensing and distilling.

He gathered the chemicals he would need: sulfur and various salts and alkalis; metals such as mercury, arsenic and antimony; acids such as aqua fortis, oil of vitriol, muriatic acid and aqua regia.

Robert still had one important bit of unfinished business. He wrote to Monsieur Marcombes. He arranged for a reunion in France to pay the debt.

Robert met with his tutor.

"I am still tutoring Boyle children," Monsieur Marcombes said. "Lord Broghill put his young sons under my care."

Robert settled his account with his former tutor. Robert explained his plans for a laboratory in the empty manor house. "My researches will be into chemistry." Robert said. "I can buy most of the equipment in England. But I need a high temperature furnace, which England cannot supply."

Monsieur Marcombes thought for a moment. He said, "Factories glaze china by placing it in a hot furnace. You'll find what you need in the Netherlands."

Robert ordered the furnace. Going home by way of London, he stayed for a few days with his sister at her new residence at Pall Mall. Eagerly, he asked about the invisible college.

"The invisible college still exists," Catharine assured him. "They meet at Dr. Jonathan Goddard's on Wood Street in Cheapside or at Gresham College.

The members welcomed Robert Boyle as an equal. The membership sounded like a roll call of England's greatest minds. Dr. Jonathan Goddard served as Oliver Cromwell's personal physician. Christopher Wren, the astronomer, also designed buildings. Dr. Isaac Barrow, a fine preacher, was also an expert mathematician. John Wallis, another churchman, cracked the code that Royalists used to send secret messages during the Civil War.

John Wilkins, the brother-in-law of Oliver Cromwell, wrote books such as *The Discovery of a World in the Moon*. People read his books for the wild speculations on one hand and solid descriptions of facts on the other. He even proposed that human beings might one day set foot on the moon. He was a courteous man with strong, broad shoulders and thick, dark hair. His mind ran in perpetual motion.

Robert Boyle told John Wilkins about his chemical researches.

"The more I study chemistry, the more confusing the subject becomes," Robert admitted. "Chemistry got off to a good start with the Egyptians. They advanced chemistry as a practical art. They learned to make glass, glaze pottery, smelt ores, dye cloth, make perfumes and cosmetics and embalm bodies. Later, the Greeks concluded that all matter is made of four basic elements: earth, water, air and fire."

John Wilkins said, "The Greek theory does seem reasonable. As a log burns in a fire, it releases water as sap, which oozes from the end. Air, or smoke, rises from the burning log. So do flames. Earth as ash is left behind. Wood contains all four elements—earth, air, fire and water.''

Robert shook his head, unconvinced. ''Alchemy grew out of the Greek view, and it has led chemistry to a dead end.''

Alchemy gained popularity during Roman times. Alchemists took the four element theory very seriously indeed. They believed that they could make gold by mixing the four elements in the right proportion. The Roman emperor Diocletian actually feared that they might successfully produce cheap gold and destroy the economy of the Empire. He ordered that alchemy books be burned.

''Laws haven't prevented alchemists from experimenting,'' Robert pointed out. ''Instead, they veil their work in mystery. They guard their discoveries closely. Reading books written by the alchemists is nearly impossible. They use secret symbols and mystical language that make sense only to themselves and their trusted assistants.''

John Wilkins quoted the alchemical motto, '''Never reveal clearly to anyone any discovery, but be sufficient unto thyself.''

Robert said, ''When I make discoveries, I shall publish them in a language that all can understand.''

Robert rode back to Stalbridge. There he put his chemical laboratory in order. He waited for delivery of his furnace. The shipment arrived from the Netherlands. Now he could begin his chemical researches in earnest.

Robert pried the packing crate apart. He unloaded the furnace. He heard something rattling inside. Robert opened the door. The fire brick, which should have lined the iron wall, lay in a crumbling heap. The thousand-mile overland journey proved too rough for the fragile fire brick. The trip damaged the furnace beyond repair.

"I must go to the Netherlands and personally bring back the furnace," Robert decided.

Frank, who had been living in Ireland, came to visit. He told Robert the sad story of his wife. "Betty lived at Stalbridge until the war came too close. Parliament imprisoned Thomas Killigrew, her brother, because of his Royalist sympathies. She escaped to The Hague."

Robert knew that many members of the royal family now lived at The Hague, the capital of the Netherlands. They still carried on an active court life.

"I've pleaded for Betty to come to Ireland to live with me," Frank said. "She thinks life there will be too dull. She is used to the sparkle and excitement of court life. I am going to The Hague for her . . . But what if she refuses? What will I do?"

Sweet Frank seldom let the cares of this world affect his easy-going nature. But Frank's problems with his wife cast a dark shadow over his cheery disposition.

Robert said, "I will go with you and help you bring Betty home."

Frank brightened. He said, "Your help is what I need."

Early in 1648 Robert and Frank went to The Hague. They hardly noticed the imposing mansions that lined the wide avenues and canals of the city. Frank had not seen his wife for seven years. The mission required all the persuasion and diplomacy he could muster. Reluctantly, Betty gave up her court life to live in Ireland.

Both Frank and Robert sailed home pleased. Frank got his wife. Robert got his chemical furnace. Frank and Betty stayed for a few days at Stalbridge before going on to Ireland.

After Frank and Betty left, Robert immersed himself in experiments. He tested the furnace. It performed flawlessly. At first he repeated the alchemical work of others. As he gained experience and confidence, he struck out into new ground. He managed the farm during the day. At night he worked in his laboratory or lay in bed and read by candlelight.

Robert was not a hermit. He led a normal country life. He fished, dined with his neighbors, and visited the local village on market day. Sometimes he would go for walks to the river, taking his fishing rod. He fly fished, using artificial lures.

Early one morning as he strolled to the river, he heard singing in a meadow. He walked closer, keeping himself hidden in the woods. A country girl kneeled on the grass beside a cow. She sang to it as she milked, quite unaware of Robert's presence. He listened for a while in secret admiration. Then he backed away, careful not to disturb her.

Robert wrote simple religious meditations while at Stalbridge. He sent these to his sister in London. Robert's writing expressed his admiration for the Creator whose hand he saw so clearly in every corner of creation.

The ideas for the essays came from ordinary events. One morning he lit a fire in the fireplace. He started the fire with small sticks, which kindled the larger logs. Robert wrote about this, pointing out that the devil works in such a way. Rather than attacking the solid core of a person's character, the devil starts small, gaining little by little.

Robert's dog, a spaniel, followed him everywhere. The little dog amused Robert. It would roam freely when in familiar territory. Yet when Robert walked to market, the spaniel followed close at his heels. The strange sights, sounds and smells frightened the animal. "With humans," Robert wrote, "it is the same. Familiar distractions and enjoyments cause them to forget and wander from their great master, but when these things fail them, they turn to cling desperately to God.''

Robert even wrote an essay about the milkmaid. ''She sang with the blushes of the morning in her cheeks, the splendor of the sun in her eyes, the freshness of the fields in her looks, the whiteness of milk expressd in her skin and the melody of the larks in her voice.'' Happiness, the girl showed, is a state of mind. Happiness doesn't depend upon one's station in life.

Although he wrote the essays for his sister, she circulated the handwritten manuscripts in London. The demand for the charming essays grew. In each one Robert described a simple observation from nature and used it to illustrate a Christian truth. Robert called them parables of nature. Eventually, Catharine collected the essays and published them as a book, *Occasional Reflections*. The book became so popular other writers tried to copy its style.

Long before Robert gained any recognition for his chemical studies, he earned wide applause for his true-to-life nature essays. When people learned that a scientist wrote the Christian devotions, they questioned him. ''Isn't there a conflict between science and faith?''

''On the contrary,'' Robert said, ''there are two chief ways to arrive at the knowledge of God: the contemplation of His works and the study of His word. I find myself oftentimes reduced to exclaim with the psalmist, 'O Lord, how manifold are thy works! in wisdom hast thou made them all.' ''

# 8

# The Gnarley Man

Late in 1648, the long running Civil War came to
an end. As Charles I tried to escape, troops trapped
him on the Isle of Wright. Parliament brought him
to London under guard. He stood trial for a variety
of charges. While others celebrated Christmas,
Charles I, the sovereign with a stutter, waited to learn
his fate. The trial ended with the dreadful sentence:
"This court doth adjudge that the said Charles Stuart,
as a tyrant, traitor, murderer and public enemy, shall
be put to death by the severing of his head from his
body."

The executioner built a scaffold out a second floor
window of the banquet hall at Windsor. Charles I lost
his head on Janauary 20, 1649. Following his death,
Parliament put the country under the protection of
Oliver Cromwell.

The Boyle family fared much better than other
Royalists under Cromwell's rule. Roger supported
Cromwell during the Civil War. Catharine talked to
members of Parliament. Cromwell and Parliament

restored the Great Earl's properties in Munster. Robert and his family once again became a rich and powerful family.

Robert received a share of the land in Ireland. He didn't greet this news with much enjoyment. He'd grown restless after living at Stalbridge for eight years. More land to oversee would take even more time from his scientific pursuits. He trekked to Ireland to see firsthand the condition of the land. He stayed with Frank at Shannon Park.

Robert confessed to his brother, "Being tied down to the farm keeps me from the weekly meetings with the invisible college, which I enjoy so much."

Frank said, "Then let me manage the estates for you."

Robert immediately agreed to the idea. He transferred ownership of his Irish estates to Frank. He put Stalbridge in the hands of a dependable caretaker (not Tom Murry!). These actions gave Robert a yearly income of 3000 pounds, more than enough to live comfortably and support his scientific researches.

In the autumn of 1654, Robert visited London. He spoke with John Wilkins about his plans. "I have decided to leave Stalbridge to live in London," Robert told his friend.

John Wilkins said, "I must urge you to settle in Oxford instead."

"Why?" Robert asked.

John Wilkins explained, "When Oliver Cromwell became Lord Protector of England, he dismissed the university leaders in Oxford. They'd been too closely tied to King Charles. Cromwell filled the vacant posts with men more to his liking. Many of the members of the invisible college received appointments to Oxford, including myself."

"Has the invisible college broken up?" Robert asked.

John Wilkins said, "We still meet, but in Oxford rather than in London. We have weekly meetings, just as we did in London. We hold our discussions in my rooms at Wadham College. You must settle in Oxford rather than London. I'll help you find the best accommodations, a place perfect for your scientific experiments."

Robert found a suite of rooms in a building owned by Mr. Crosse, an apothecary. The house was on High Street, next to University College.

Although Robert Boyle would live in Oxford, he did not plan to attend the university. It was just as well. Universities ignored modern science. A hundred years had passed since Copernicus proposed his theory that the earth revolved around the sun as one of the planets. Yet, universities ignored that theory in favor of the older earth-centered theory of Ptolemy. The telescopic discoveries of Galileo, the magnetic discoveries of Gilbert and the astronomical discoveries of Kepler found no place in the teachings at Oxford or most other universities.

Robert said good-bye to the country life. He left behind the gardens and orchards, the fly fishing, and the milkmaid who sang to her cows. He entered the world of science full time.

In June of 1654, a horse-drawn wagon rumbled down High Street and stopped in front of Mr. Crosse's apothecary. Workmen heaved and grunted as they unloaded the wagon and carried the smaller trunks up the stairs. The heavy crates they hoisted by a block and tackle through a second story window.

At age 27, Robert Boyle moved into his new residence at Oxford. At last he fulfilled his dream of being a full-time experimental scientist. He set up a complete laboratory in his suite. Some of the chemical equipment came from Stalbridge. The rest he purchased in London.

John Wilkins watched as Robert directed the workmen. "You have one of the best laboratories I have ever seen," he said.

Robert said, "I want to staff it with the best assistants I can find. I have asked Mr. Peter Stahl to serve as the chemical tutor to both myself and my laboratory assistants. I'm determined to learn as much as I can about practical chemistry. Mr. Stahl will instruct my staff in how to use the apparatus and the proper way to handle chemicals."

"Mr. Stahl is a talented man," John Wilkins agreed. "Have you assembled the rest of your assistants?"

Robert Boyle said, "Not completely. I wish to employ a bright young man to serve as head laboratory assistant and instrument maker."

Thoughtfully John Wilkins said, "Most students at Oxford come from wealthy families. They have no need to earn money for their education. However, there is one deserving student name Robert Hooke. His parents died when he was 13, leaving him an orphan. He earns a living by waiting on the tables of the other students."

"Tell me more about him," Robert Boyle said.

John Wilkins said, "Robert Hooke was the son of a country preacher. His parents despaired of him reaching school age because of repeated bouts of sickness. He did survive, although his frail health kept him out of regular school. He is a mechanical genius. As a youngster he made his own toys—toy ships that would sail, toy cannons that would go off, and toy clocks that kept time."

"Young Mr. Hooke appears to fit my requirements perfectly," Robert Boyle said.

John Wilkins said, "He is a peculiar individual. His constant battles with disease have left his figure frail and badly crippled. His legs and arms are shrunken. His hair hangs in uncombed locks over his face, which is twisted by constant headaches and pain. He seldom sleeps, probably because of the pain. Instead, he takes short cat naps at odd moments.''

"What of his scientific ability?" Robert Boyle asked.

John Wilkins said, "He is a remarkably clever individual. No one doubts his talent as a scientist. Do you remember my book *A New World in the Moon?* I speculated about travel to the moon. Mr. Hooke came up with thirty proposals for ways to fly through air.''

"I must speak with Mr. Hooke," Robert Boyle decided.

John Wilkins said, "Some people find Mr. Hooke to be argumentative, quarrelsome and short-tempered.''

Robert Boyle remembered Monsieur Marcombes's quick temper. "If the ability is there, other faults can be overlooked. Please ask Mr. Robert Hooke to see me at his convenience.''

Late that evening, the young man knocked at Robert's door.

The small, twisted man quick-stepped into the room. Mr. Hooke, only twenty years old, looked years older. He had a pale, almost white, face. He seldom stood still. He spoke so quickly the words fell upon one another.

"Good evening Mr. Boyle," the young man said. "What can I do for you?"

Robert Boyle looked with sympathy at the young man. He recalled trees that grew along the coast of Ireland. Rocky soil stunted their growth. Constant storms twisted their limbs. The painful condition of Mr. Hooke reminded Robert Boyle of those pitiful, twisted trees.

"Well, Mr. Boyle," Mr. Hooke said impatiently, "what do you want of me?"

"Have you heard of the invisible college?" Robert asked.

"The men of the new learning. Yes, yes, I have," Mr. Hooke said. He paced the room, his hands touching the laboratory equipment. His eyes darted about, bright and shining below the dark locks of hair over his forehead.

"We talk about many things of science," Robert Boyle said. "At the last meeting I learned of an exciting experiment carried out by Otto von Guericke, mayor of Magdenburg, Germany. He designed and built an air pump. With it he could pump air out of a container."

"Yes, I've studied the experiment," Mr. Hooke said impatiently. "He made two copper bowls, each about two feet across. The bowls fitted together to form a sphere. He filled the seam around them with wax to make them airtight. Then he pumped out most of the air through a pipe attached to one of the hemispheres. Guericke hooked an eight-horse team to each half of the sphere. The teams pulled in opposite directions. They couldn't pull the hemispheres apart. He opened the valve and let air inside the hemisphere. They fell apart."

Robert Boyle said, "Aristotle and those scientists who agree with him would say that the vacuum inside the hemispheres held them together. I say it was nothing *inside* the hemispheres that held them together. Instead, the pressure of air *outside* forced the hemispheres together. Letting air into the globe equalized the outside and inside air pressure. The two copper bowls fell apart."

"So?" Mr. Hooke asked.

Robert Boyle said, "An air pump is an important

scientific device, as important as the telescope. I must have an air pump of my own.''

"You want me to build one?'' Mr. Hooke asked.

"Yes, but an improved model,'' Robert Boyle said. "Guericke's pump is only a modified water pump. He began by trying to pump the water out of a wine cast. He thought this would leave a vacuum. Later, he discovered he could pump air out directly. His design is clumsy. He must operate the pump underwater to keep air from leaking in. In addition, he used copper bowls. I want a clear glass bowl so we can see inside as the air is pumped out.''

Mr. Hooke paced the room. He built something in his mind. "Yes,'' he said at last. "I see how it would work.''

Robert Boyle said, "I've asked another instrument maker to build an air pump. He has met with failure so far. If you succeed before he does, then the position is yours.''

"Yes, yes,'' Mr. Hooke said, lost in thought. He began clearing a table. "I'll stay here and work on it if you don't mind.''

"It is past bed time,'' Robert Boyle said.

Without looking up, Mr. Hooke said, "I have no bed time.''

Mr. Hooke's pump, although quickly built and crudely made, performed much better than any others in existence.

With obvious and honest pride, Mr. Hooke showed the device in operation. He explained to Robert Boyle how it worked. "Brass pipes connect pistons and pump barrels to the glass receiver. Oiled leather valves at the end of the pistons let air pass one way but not the other. The pump forms a vacuum in the glass receiver.''

"What is the capacity of the receiver?'' Robert Boyle asked.

"About eight gallons," Robert Hooke said. "A hole in the bottom of the receiver connects to the pump. The hole at the top allows you to insert objects inside the receiver. Once inside, you seal the top hole with a tight-fitting stopper."

"You did well, Robert Boyle said. "The pump is a marvel."

Almost as soon as he finished the first pump, Mr. Hooke started work on a second and even better one. "I'd like to replace the glass receiver with a bell-shaped one, with a large open base. Such a design will allow you to place large objects inside. The bell jar will rest on a metal plate and be sealed with wax. Also, I can put a shut-off valve in the brass pipe to keep air from leaking back in."

"We'll have time to improve it later," Robert Boyle promised the young man. "For now I'm anxious to begin a series of experiments on air pressure. I'll choose simple experiments and describe them in detail. Others can repeat them and check our results."

As a quick test of the air pump, Robert Boyle filled a soft, elastic animal bladder with air and then tied it closed. He placed the balloonlike bladder inside and plugged the receiver. Assistants raised and lowered the pump arm.

With every downstroke of the piston, air left the receiver. The bladder began to swell. It doubled in size. Suddenly it burst.

Satisfied, Robert Boyle offered an explanation for what he observed. "Normally, the bladder didn't expand because the pressure of the air inside it equals the pressure of the air in the receiver. As we removed the air in the receiver, this reduces the pressure, allowing the air in the bladder to expand. Eventually, it expanded so much that it burst."

Robert Boyle wrote a list of things to try. "I wonder if a candle will burn in a vacuum?"

He lighted a candle and lowered it by a thin wire into the receiver. Then he put the stopper in and waited for the candle to go out.

"When you put a burning candle in a closed vessel

the flame goes out anyway,'' Mr. Hooke said. ''The air becomes stale.''

Robert Boyle continued to watch the burning candle, measuring the time. The receiver filled with smoke. Finally, after five minutes, the candle flame dimmed and went out.

Robert Boyle opened the receiver and let in fresh air. He relit the candle and once again lowered it into the receiver. This time his assistants immediately began pumping out the air. The flame burned for less than a minute.

''The flame goes out much sooner when it has no air,'' Robert observed. ''Air, or something in the air, is necessary for burning.'' He noticed something else. ''Smoke rises in air, but in a vacuum it falls to the bottom of the receiver!''

Robert Boyle numbered his experiments. For experiment number 16 he tested whether a magnet could act through a vacuum. He put a compass inside the glass receiver. When he brought a magnet near the outside wall, it attracted the compass needle. Next he pumped out the air and tried again. The magnet attracted the compass needle as before.

''It is plain,'' Robert Boyle said, ''that magnetic forces can cut through a vacuum.''

''So can light,'' Mr. Hooke pointed out. ''Look at objects through a vacuum and compare how they look with air in the receiver. They are just as bright either way. Apparently light can travel in a vacuum, just like magnetic forces.''

''Humm,'' Robert Boyle said. ''Is it truly a void inside the glass? How can light travel through nothing? What about sound? Can it travel in a vacuum?''

Mr. Hooke owned a large watch that ticked loudly. He took off the case so they could see the clockwork rock back and forth inside. He tied a thin string to

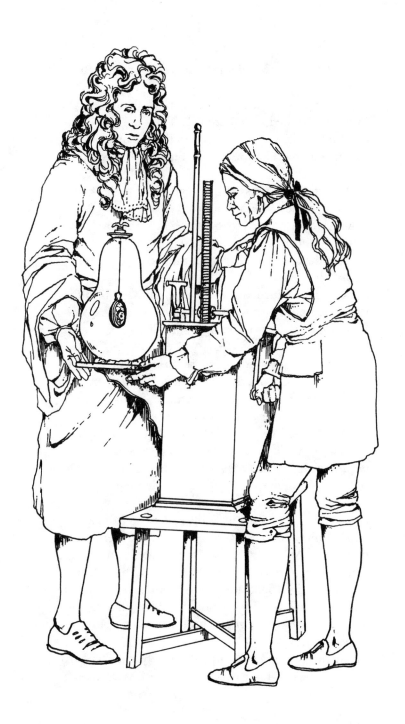

the watch and lowered it into the receiver. He sealed it with a stopper.

"I can hear it ticking from here," Robert Boyle said. He listened to the *tick-tick*. They began pumping out the air, stopping now and then to listen to the watch. The sound grew fainter. Finally, they couldn't hear it.

Robert Boyle pressed his head against the glass. "Not a sound," he announced.

Mr. Hooke pointed to the watch mechanism. "The watch is still running," he said.

"Let the air slowly back into the receiver," Robert Boyle directed.

Mr. Hooke turned the valve. Air hissed into the receiver. Faintly, they heard the ticking again. With the air completely restored, it sounded as loud as it had in the beginning.

"Light and sound must be fundamentally different," Robert Boyle concluded. "Light travels through a vacuum without hindrance. Sound doesn't carry unless there is air in the receiver."

"What shall we do next?" Mr. Hooke asked.

Robert Boyle said, "We should repeat our experiments in the presence of members of the invisible college. I'll invite them to hold their next meeting here."

The members of the invisible college welcomed the opportunity to see Robert Boyle's experiments firsthand. All of the regulars attended, including Christopher Wren. He'd obtained his master's degree at Oxford in 1653. He lectured in astronomy at Gresham College. He was a remarkably brilliant man, one who enjoyed good health and a cheerful disposition.

For the important group, Robert Boyle and Mr. Hooke repeated their experiments with the burning candle, the ticking watch, the magnet and compass. Everything worked flawlessly.

Christopher Wren spoke for all of the scientists in the room. "We are indeed pleased to be present at such an important moment in the history of science. Your air pump, Mr. Boyle, will be counted as a great invention. It has opened so many doors for investigation."

"Thank you," Robert Boyle said. "But do not call it my air pump. Mr. Hooke designed it and built it. He, and he alone, deserves all the credit for its construction. Call it Mr. Hooke's air pump. His wonderful invention makes it possible to carry out experiments never dreamed possible before."

To conclude the evening, Robert Boyle planned his most dramatic experiment of all.

"At Eton I first learned of Galileo's thought experiment of dropping a coin and a feather at the same time in a vacuum. Galileo argued that both would fall at the same speed," Robert Boyle said. "At the time, neither he nor any other scientist thought the experiment could be done. Now it can."

Robert Boyle had ordered his glass blowers to fashion a glass tube several feet long. He placed a lump of lead and a feather inside. He stoppered it tightly and attached the other end to the air pump. Once the pump had done its job, Robert closed the shut-off valve. He lifted the glass tube, which contained a vacuum. The lump of lead and feather rested at the bottom.

"Watch this!" Robert said. Quickly he turned the glass tube upside down.

Lead and feather fell side by side.

His guests applauded. They shook his hand, gave him a hearty slap on his back. With parting congratulations they bid him good night.

Robert Boyle closed the door after they left. He stood in the silence of his laboratory. After eight years of trying, after eight years of painful delays, and learning his craft little by little, he realized tonight marked a turning point in his life.

As a scientist, he had arrived.

# 9

# The Spring of the Air

At Oxford, Robert Boyle pursued scientific studies other than chemistry. He dissected fish and studied anatomy. He collected recipes for medical remedies. He studied the operation of an air rifle that shot a projectile by compressed air. He learned how to grind and polish glass lenses for telescopes and microscopes.

During these exciting days, the Oxford invisibles came to Robert's laboratory to see the latest wonders. The three most frequent visitors were Christopher Wren, John Wilkins and Dr. Seth Ward.

One evening discussions turned to the weight of the air. Until the time of Galileo in the early 1600's, people ignored the atmosphere. They didn't think of air as an actual substance. Instead, they thought of air as a mysterious spirit.

Dr. Seth Ward asked, "Does air have weight?"

"I'm certain that it does," Robert Boyle said.

Christopher Wren agreed, "Doubtless you are right, although no one has ever directly weighed a container filled with air and the same container empty of air."

"Other experimenters didn't have an air pump,"
Robert Boyle said. "Let me think upon the problem."

At last he devised an experiment that would settle
the matter. He explained it to Robert Hooke.
"Weighing air will be a delicate and difficult task. I've
ordered from the glass blowers a glass bulb the size
of a hen's egg with a narrow stem at one end. We'll
seal the stem with wax so the air in the glass bulb is
trapped, even when placed inside the vacuum
receiver."

The quick-witted Robert Hooke instantly saw what
they would have to do. He said, "We'll place the glass
bulb on a small pan scale inside the receiver. We'll
balance tiny weights in one side of the balance against
the glass bulb on the other side."

They had to open the receiver, change the weights,
reseal the receiver and pump out the air. Little by little, they added weights to the pan. Finally, bulb and
weights balanced.

"All right," Robert Boyle said. "Remove the glass
bulb from the receiver and punch a hole in the sealing wax. Then put it back in the receiver and start
the air pump."

This time the pump removed the air from both the
receiver and the bulb. The side of the balance scale
with the weights fell, showing that side to be heavier.
The glass bulb weighed more with air in it than with
the air pumped out of it.

"This is the first direct proof that air has weight,"
Robert Boyle reported to the invisible college.

Dr. Seth Ward asked, "How much does the air
weigh?"

"The air in the glass bulb weighed a tiny amount,
less than two grains," Robert Boyle said. "I estimate
that a cubic foot of air weighs between one and two
ounces."

Christopher Wren said, "Such a weight is about a thousand times less than an equal volume of water. No wonder scientists have argued about whether air had weight."

Robert Boyle was not the first scientist to investigate the atmosphere. That honor belonged to Evangelista Torricelli. He served as Galileo's assistant during the last three years of Galileo's life. Torricelli invented the *barometer*, a device that measures air pressure.

Evangelista Torricelli began with a long glass tube open at one end and closed at the other. He filled the tube with mercury. He capped the open end of the tube with his finger and up-ended the tube in a dish of mercury. He removed his finger. The mercury partially drained from the tube, leaving a vacuum at the top of the tube. A column of mercury 30 inches high stood in the tube.

Exactly why the mercury column remained in the tube caused endless arguments among scientists. Some said the vacuum at the top of the tube pulled the mercury up from the dish. Evangelista Torricelli thought otherwise. He believed the outside air pressing down on the mercury in the open dish forced the mercury up the tube.

Robert Boyle agreed with Evangelista Torricelli's conclusion. "Two forces are at work in the barometer. One is the weight of the mercury in the tube. The other is the weight of the air upon the mercury in the dish. Mercury drains from the tube until its own weight equals the atmospheric pressure. A barometer measures air pressure," Robert said.

Most of the other members of the invisible college agreed that the weight of the air supported the column of mercury.

Christopher Wren said, "Atmospheric pressure decreases as you climb higher in the atmosphere."

"How do you know?" Robert Boyle asked.

Christopher Wren told about Blaise Pascal, a French scientist. "In 1648, he wondered how the mercury level of a barometer would change if carried up a mountain. Pascal himself was in delicate health. He designed the experiment, but he let his brother-in-law, Florent Perier, carry it out. Pascal gave his brother-in-law a barometer. He sent Florent Perier up the side of Pay-de-Dome, a tall mountain in central France. Florent Perier measured air pressure at the base of the mountain and at a height of one mile. He found that the mercury column fell by three inches due to the lower air pressure at the greater height."

"Three inches is one tenth of its original height," Robert Boyle said. "This means that about one tenth of the atmosphere lies below one mile. How certain are we that the experiment is correct?"

Christopher Wren said, "I have repeated the experiment in London. I used a tall building rather than a mountain. I measured the height of a barometer at street level. Then I carried the barometer up the stairs to the top of the bell tower at St. Mary's. The barometer level fell slightly, not much, but noticeably."

"Pascal did his experiment more than 10 years ago," Robert Boyle said. "It has taken all that time for word of it to become generally known in the scientific community. Something must be done to help scientists learn of each other's work more quickly."

"Our friend Henry Oldenburg has an idea," Christopher Wren said. "He acts as a clearing house for new ideas. Scientists write directly to him. They describe their experiments. He reads their letters and condenses what he has learned. Then he writes letters to other scientists all over England and Europe. In this way, a single letter reaches dozens of scientists.

Even so, it is a slow and clumsy way to communicate new learning."

Henry Oldenburg, a Puritan, dressed in the traditional black and white garb. He was a German by birth, although he received an education at Oxford. Henry Oldenburg scratched for money. He served as the London agent for German businessmen. He tutored students, including Dick Jones, one of Catharine's sons. He also earned money by writing rough notes into finished manuscripts.

"I employ Henry Oldenburg to transcribe my notes," Robert Boyle said. "The man's penmanship is flawless."

Robert presented his notes in rough form. Henry Oldenburg wrote them out in clear hand. Robert Boyle then circulated the notes among the invisible college. "After I receive comments about the manuscript, I will have it printed," Robert Boyle said.

Henry Oldenburg lived in London. He visited Oxford to enroll the young Dick Jones in school.

"What title shall I use for your book about the air?" Henry Oldenburg asked.

"Call it *New Experiments* for now," Robert Boyle told him.

Henry Oldenburg urged Robert Boyle to send the manuscript pages to London by a personal servant. "The quality of parcel post service is a disgrace," Henry Oldenburg said. "Coachmen charge double for mail packages, and then lose them."

Robert Boyle sought out ingenious experiments for his book. He managed to put a mercury barometer inside the receiver of his pump. The top of the barometer tube extended above the receiver. Robert Boyle sealed the opening with wax to make the opening air tight.

As his assistants pumped the air out of the receiver, the barometer fell.

"It is just as if I'd taken the barometer to the top of a high mountain," Robert Boyle remarked. "Continue to pump. Let's see how far it will fall."

The men pumped for fifteen minutes. The assistants breathed heavily from hard effort. Robert Boyle called a halt. The assistants fell back, exhausted. A half inch of mercury still remained in the tube.

One assistant asked, "Why does it still stay in the tube?"

Robert Boyle explained, "The air pump can't produce a perfect vacuum. The small amount of air remaining in the receiver is enough to support the last half inch of mercury."

Even so, the results made Robert Boyle quite happy. He said, "This proves conclusively what I have believed all along. The pressure of the atmosphere, not the suction of a vacuum, supports the mercury in a barometer tube."

To satisfy himself still further, he let air back into the receiver little by little. The moment he opened the valve, the mercury rose in the tube. Finally, with the air fully restored to the receiver, the mercury regained its original level.

For a long time people had known that even the best water pumps couldn't lift water higher than 34 feet. These experiments helped Robert Boyle discover the reason.

Robert Boyle realized that a water pump raises water by pumping air from the pipe. The pressure of the outside air forces water up the pipe. When the weight of the water in the pipe equals the weight of the atmosphere, the water can rise no further.

Robert decided to demonstrate the action of a water pump. He had several tin pipes, each about an inch in diameter, soldered together to make a tube 32 feet long. The pipe ended with a glass tube about three

feet long. He connected the tube to his air pump. He selected a four-story house and placed a tank of water in the street outside. He put the pump on the roof of the house. The tin pipe extended from the tank of water to the top of the roof.

Onlookers gathered in the street to watch.

"As we pump out the air, water will rise in the pipe," Robert Boyle told them. "The last section, made of glass, will let us see the height of the water."

"How high will the water rise in the pipe?" one interested bystander asked.

Robert calculated what to expect. "A mercury barometer is 30 inches high. Mercury is 13.5 times heavier than water. A water barometer would be 13.5 times higher than a mercury barometer. That works out to be 405 inches, or about 34 feet. A perfect air pump should be able to lift the water to that height."

His assistants began pumping. Up and down they cranked the piston. The water rose in the pipe. Finally, Robert Boyle could see the water through the glass. The water rose to 33 feet and six inches, but no higher.

Satisfied, Robert Boyle called a halt to the experiment. "The water doesn't rise the final six inches because the pump cannot make a perfect vacuum. Even a perfect pump would be unable to get it higher than 34 feet."

This experiment also allowed Robert Boyle to estimate the thickness of the ocean of air around the earth. "Water weighs a thousand times more than the same volume of air. The atmosphere must be a thousand times higher than the column of water, or about 34,000 feet high, almost seven miles."

He realized that the total height of the atmosphere would be much greater. The upper layers would have less air pressing down on them. Because of the reduced pressure, they would spread out to an even greater height.

In 1657, Henry Oldenburg and young Dick Jones left England for a one-year tour of the continent.

Robert Boyle told them, "Please remember to write often. Keep me informed of what is new and interesting in the scientific world."

Henry Oldenburg did write. In one letter he reported that European scientists believed they could use the barometer to predict the weather. "A steady, high barometer signals the onset of fair weather. A rapidly falling barometer means a storm is approaching."

Could such an astonishing idea be true, Robert Boyle wondered. He discussed the matter with Christopher Wren. Robert Boyle said, "Air pressure isn't constant. The height of the mercury in a barometer does change slightly from day to day."

Christopher Wren said, "It may be possible that changes in the weather cause changes in air pressure."

Robert Boyle said, "I'll follow the weather and compare it with the barometer."

Mr. Hooke offered to record the barometer reading each day. He practically lived in the laboratory. Once, Robert came into the laboratory early in the morning. He found the young scientist asleep on a bed of straw in the corner under a table. Mr. Hooke could only sleep when exhaustion overcame the feverish activity of his mind. As Robert Boyle looked upon the young man, his frail body shook. He moaned as if having a bad dream. Mr. Hooke awoke. He'd slept for only a few minutes.

Robert Boyle marveled at the brilliant inventor's ability to overcome such trying circumstances. Other people found Mr. Hooke short-tempered and sharp-tongued. Robert Boyle, however, stayed on good terms with the young scientist.

Robert Boyle took pains to give credit to Robert

Hooke for his part in the discoveries. "I'm pleased with the performance of Mr. Hooke's air pump," Robert Boyle told the invisibles. "It misses making a perfect vacuum by only a small amount."

Although the two scientists worked together on some projects, they also pursued ideas separately. During the last few months, Mr. Hooke had taken up the microscope. He studied its design and built a better one. He viewed insects, feathers, fish scales and tiny pieces of wood through the improved microscope.

"Look at this," Mr. Hooke said.

Robert looked through the microscope and examined the object on the stage. "What is it?" Robert asked. "It has a repeated, regular pattern."

Mr. Hooke explained, "You are looking at a thin slice of cork. The pattern reminds me of a series of tiny rooms. I've found tiny building blocks like the ones you see in most living substances. I call them cells."

While Mr. Hooke peered into his microscope, Robert Boyle began an exciting study into the spring of the air. When air is compressed and then released, it tends to spring back to it original volume. He ordered a large glass tube shaped like the letter **J**. The top of the short end was closed. The top of the long end opened out into a funnel. Overall, the glass tube stood seventeen feet high.

Robert poured mercury into the tube. It trapped air in the short, closed part of the tube. Pouring in additional mercury compressed the air in the short end more and more.

"Air resists changes in volume," Robert Boyle explained to Mr. Hooke. "I have found a simple law to summarize the relationship between volume and pressure. Doubling the pressure on a gas compresses it to one-half its original volume. Tripling the pressure on a gas compresses it to one-third its original size. On the other hand, when the pressure is relieved, the gas springs back to its original volume."

Boyle cooled the trapped, compressed air with a wet cloth and warmed it with a candle flame. He noticed that small changes in the volume resulted. Air expanded when heated and contracted when cooled.

His discovery, known as *Boyle's Law*, states that volume and pressure of a gas are inversely related. As one increases the other decreases in a predictable way, provided temperature remains constant. It was the first physical law to describe the action of the atmosphere. The atmosphere, rather than being a mysterious substance, followed natural laws like any other physical substance.

Robert Boyle changed the title of his book to *New Experiments Touching on the Spring of the Air*. He put the book into final form and sent it to his London printer. The book created a sensation when it was published.

Both natural philosophers and ordinary citizens bought the book and read it.

What made the book so successful? Robert Boyle chose to write an easy-to-read style. Rather than trying to impress people by using difficult language, he instead chose simple language. The book began with a detailed description of Mr. Hooke's air pump. He then described 43 experiments carried out with the apparatus. The experiments, not quotes from ancient authorities, made up the heart of the book. He described his experiments, summarized his discoveries and explained their importance.

In addition, Robert Boyle had to correct mistaken ideas held by his readers. Yet, he knew that adults often resented being corrected. Robert Boyle developed a way to overcome this. He pretended to aim his book to his nephew, young Dick Jones. In that way he could present it in a language simple enough for adults to understand.

In London, a government employee named Samuel Pepys bought the book. Samuel Pepys kept a day-to-day diary of the important events that happened in London. He recorded the publication of *New Experiments* as one of those important events. Samuel Pepys wasn't a scientist. But the book so impressed him he sought out the London invisible college and began meeting with them.

Robert Boyle traveled to London shortly after the publication of his book. The London invisibles met at Gresham College. Robert Boyle attended one of their meetings.

Samuel Pepys rushed forward to greet Robert Boyle. "I shall eagerly buy every one of your books as you issue them," he promised. "Even I can understand your writing."

Robert Boyle said, "I always esteem the author who

does not try to show his own learning but tries to increase the knowledge of his reader. Scientific progress depends upon scientists informing the world of their discoveries. In this way, one scientist can build on the work of another.''

''You make the study of nature seem so simple,'' Samuel Pepys said.

Robert Boyle explained, ''God would not have made the universe as it is unless he intended us to understand it.''

Scientists around the world heaped praise upon Robert Boyle. When Robert Boyle learned of Galileo's death, he wondered who would replace that great scientist. Most people hailed Robert Boyle as the successor to Galileo.

# 10

# The Royal Society

For Robert Boyle, each triumph in his laboratory confirmed his conviction that the world of nature was the handiwork of the Creator. He devoted himself to an in-depth study of the Bible. He studied Hebrew and Greek, so he could read the Scriptures in those ancient languages. Part of Daniel and a few other portions of Scripture were written in Syriac. He took pains to understand that tongue.

Business matters took Robert Boyle to London. While there he met with James Ussher, an Irish scholar. The man had served as archbishop of Armagh. When the Civil War started, James Ussher came to England, living first at Oxford. Then he moved to London as preacher at Lincoln's Inn.

James Ussher believed he could find enough clues in the Bible to establish the date of creation. He studied all the references to dates and ages in the Old Testament. By carefully listing all the people and adding their ages, he concluded that God created Adam in the year 4004 B.C.

Robert Boyle admired the famous Bible scholar. The two men talked about their study of Bible languages.

"I could find no teacher of Syriac," Robert Boyle said, "nor any person who so much as knew the characters of the alphabet. I learned the language with no other living teacher but God and myself."

James Ussher said, "People expect members of the clergy to master the Bible. Your skill at Scripture would put many of them to shame."

Robert Boyle expressed impatience with people too lazy to study the Bible. He said, "Some people expect to obtain from God the knowledge of His book as easily as Adam did a wife—by sleeping and having her presented to him at his awakening."

James Ussher said, "We are fortunate to have English as our native language. We have the King James Translation. We have study aids such as Bible commentaries and atlases. All of these are in English. Many people have no translation of the Bible in their own language."

Robert Boyle tried to imagine life without the Bible.

James Ussher continued, "There is no Arab Bible, none for the Indians of North America or for the island natives of the East Indies. Even the Irish have no Gaelic translation of the Bible."

Few of the Irish read English. Most spoke Gaelic, the native tongue of Ireland. Thoughtfully, Robert Boyle asked, "What would be the expenses involved in making a Gaelic Bible?"

James Ussher said, "The translation is only the first step. The book would have to be printed and distributed. It would be an expensive undertaking. The total cost for five hundred copies would be three or four thousand pounds."

Robert Boyle felt special affection for the Irish. He

wanted to help them. He didn't have enough money
to pay for an Irish Bible, or even to hire someone to
begin the translation. However, he didn't entirely
forget the matter.

Robert Boyle returned to the laboratory. He had
become England's best known scientist and one of the
most famous scientists in the world.

Events outside of his laboratory were not as
pleasant. Oliver Cromwell strengthened his control
of the country at the expense of personal liberty. When
Oliver Cromwell first took office, he allowed people
to express views that differed from his own. As time
passed, it became difficult to personally disagree with
him. His power became almost total. Oliver Cromwell
never wore a crown, but he took on all the powers
of a king.

Oliver Cromwell suffered from malaria. In August
of 1658, the alternate chills and fevers of the disease
sent him to bed. On the Sunday of August 29,
churches all over England held a special prayer service for his recovery.

The next morning, Monday, Robert awoke to find
the barometer at the lowest reading he'd ever seen.
He tapped the tube. He hardly believed the reading,
down to 27 inches. Such a low reading predicted bad
weather.

A few hours later a powerful storm swept across
England. All day the storm raged. The winds howled.
People fled inside their homes. They closed the shut-
ters and huddled in the cellars. The storm ripped off
roofs. It uprooted trees.

Robert Boyle stayed calm. He'd survived the terrible storm in the Swiss Alps. He expected this one to
leave him untouched, too. He watched the barometer.
It began rising again. The storm blew itself out.

Robert Boyle was not the only one to do scientific

experiments as the winds howled. In Lincolnshire, a sixteen-year-old boy jumped first with the wind and then against it. The boy calculated the force of the wind from the difference in the distances. The boy lived at an old manor house at Woolsthorpe. His name was Isaac Newton.

Superstitious people believed the storm predicted some dire event. Their fears were confirmed when Oliver Cromwell's condition worsened. Three days later he died.

Many of Robert Boyle's friends trembled at the news. They owed their positions at Oxford to Cromwell. They had supported him when he came into power.

"He rewarded us with the jobs we now hold," Seth Ward said. "What will happen to us now that Cromwell is dead?"

"Richard Cromwell will take his place," Robert Boyle said.

John Wilkins said, "He is a dismal choice. Richard will rule simply because he is Oliver's son. Everyone knows that he can't govern the country."

Richard Cromwell was a weak ruler. The army refused to follow his orders. Parliament turned against him. Richard Cromwell watched helplessly as his government collapsed. Opposing groups armed themselves.

Roger Boyle, the eldest Boyle, sent for his brothers to come to Ireland. Roger said, "I have supported Richard Cromwell as long as possible. His power is crumbling. Civil war threatens again."

Frank whispered a prayer. "Lord have mercy on us."

Robert asked, "What do you intend to do?"

Roger said, "Only one course of action is open to us. We must work for the return of Charles II."

Charles II, son of Charles I lived in Holland.

The brothers discussed the matter. At last, they agreed with Roger, who wrote a letter to Charles II. The letter detailed how the Boyle family would help restore the monarchy to England. Frank volunteered to carry the letter to Holland. Other royalists in England made secret trips to Holland, too.

In May of 1660, the royalists formed a delegation of the leading citizens in England. They crossed the English Channel to escort Charles II back to England. Robert Boyle joined them in a dual role. He represented the Great Earl of Cork's family and the world of science.

On May 25, the delegation returned to England. They landed in Dover with Charles II. Four days later they arrived in London. Most people had grown weary of the strife. They welcomed Charles II. Enthusiastic crowds lined the streets and leaned out of windows and balconies. They threw flowers along the way. The bells of the city rang out. Trumpets sounded. Twenty thousand soldiers raised their swords in allegiance as Charles II entered Whitehall.

Once back in England, Robert visited his sister Catharine in London. He viewed the return of the king with satisfaction. "I am certain the restoration will take place smoothly and peacefully. We have avoided another bloody civil war."

Catharine expressed mixed feelings. "Since the early days of the Long Parliament, Cromwell's supporters have met at my house. My friends opposed the return of Charles. What will he do to them?"

"You'll be safe. Charles wants to bring peace to England," Robert said. "Roger tells me that the King is a true politician. He'll reward his friends and bribe his enemies. The Boyle family has nothing to fear from Charles."

"What of our friend John Milton?" Catharine asked. "He worked closely with Cromwell for several years. His stand against Charles II has put his life in real danger. Parliament has issued a warrant for his arrest."

Robert Boyle knew that the writer had gone totally blind. Robert asked, "Where is he?"

"No one knows," she said. "He has disappeared from his home and gone into hiding."

Robert Boyle looked closely at his sister. Robert knew that she occasionally visited John Milton and read to him. Could she have been the one who guided the blind man to a safe hiding place?

Catharine said, "Please help save him. His mind is too precious for us to lose to the hangman's noose."

John Milton's friends, including the Boyle family, spoke privately with the King's advisors. They counseled against harsh actions. Although Charles II did dismiss some of his most violent critics from their posts, he promised religious tolerance. He issued a general pardon for Cromwell's followers. He dropped the proceedings against John Milton.

The poet came out of hiding. He'd concealed himself in the house of a friend in Bartholomew Close. This was a narrow passage, entered from West Smithfield under an old archway. London buzzed with the news of John Milton's deliverance.

The Boyle family took part in the festival conferring the monarchy upon Charles II. Shortly after that, the King rewarded Roger with the title of Earl of Orrery. Frank became a Privy Councilor, a private advisor to Charles II.

Charles II sent a man to work out a suitable reward for Robert Boyle. "As you know," the man said, "his Majesty desires to reward those who have supported the restoration of the monarchy. He wishes to offer you a peerage."

If Robert Boyle accepted the offer, he would become a nobleman, with a title such as duke, earl or baron. Mentally, he reviewed the honors held by his family. Each of his brothers were peers. Of his eight sisters, one had married a viscount, three had married earls, two married lords, and one a knight.

Robert said, "My father would have been proud of his sons. England has showered honors upon the Boyle family. My brothers and sisters have received enough honors for the entire family. I see little personal value in having the title of duke or earl. I enjoy all the privileges of wealth and rank. Express to King

Charles my happiness to be considered for this honor, but tell him that I decline it."

The King's man did not give up. "His Majesty is well aware of your religious knowledge and dedication to the service of Christianity. He has authorized me to offer you a high church post."

The offer surprised Robert Boyle. He'd never hidden his religious conviction. Yet, He'd never expected it to come to the attention of the King.

The King's man pressed ahead. "Will you accept a position in the church?"

"No-o-o," Robert Bole said slowly.

"On what grounds?" the man said.

Robert Boyle said, "Some people are not interested in serving God. They fortify themselves against sermons by saying that the clergy preach because they are paid to do so. As a private citizen I will have more impact for Christianity than as a church official."

The man threw up his hands. "I must say that you are a difficult man to satisfy. King Charles charged me with finding a suitable reward for you. How can I do that if you refuse all offers?"

Robert Boyle said, "I am quite satisfied with my current station in life."

The man made one last attempt. "The Provost of Eton is available. Would you accept that post?"

Robert Boyle could not reject this offer as quickly as the others. Robert Boyle counted Sir Henry Wotton as one of the great inspirations during his education. By taking the same post as Sir Henry Wotton, could he influence other young people? Finally, however, Robert Boyle declined that attractive post, too.

"I have chosen my way of life," Robert Boyle said. "Public office is but a glittering kind of slavery."

The King's man walked away shaking his head. Robert Boyle could have been a peer. He could have

been a bishop. He could have accepted a high government post. Yet, Robert Boyle wished to remain simply
Mr. Robert Boyle, a Christian gentleman.

Robert Boyle told his sister, "My concern is not
public office, but the invisible college. It has fallen
upon hard times."

"What is the matter with it?" Catharine asked.

Robert explained, "The invisible college has never
been a strong, formal organization. We meet
whenever the members feel like it. We keep no
membership list and collect no dues. The invisible
college has no rules to regulate its activity. The disrup-
tions of the last two years have played havoc with the
Oxford group."

"What do you mean?" Catharine asked.

"The Oxford group no longer meets," Robert said.
"A couple of years ago, two of our most important
members moved away. Christopher Wren became
professor of astronomy at Gresham College here in
London. John Wilkins received the post of Master of
Trinity College in Cambridge. The political distur-
bances during the restoration of the Crown scattered
my friends even more. Seth Ward, for one, lost his
post at Oxford."

"What about the invisible college in London?"
Catharine asked.

Robert said, "I shall meet with Christopher Wren
to learn its fate."

On the afternoon of November 28, 1660, Robert
Boyle and a few other natural philosophers gathered
at Gresham College in a brick-and-timber house on
Basinghall Street. Robert Boyle questioned
Christopher Wren about the London invisibles.

"We have fared no better than the Oxford group,"
Christopher Wren reported. "We disbanded when the
military took over our quarters last year."

"The soldiers have gone for now," Robert Boyle said. "We must revive the invisible college. We should have an official organization, one with formal rules."

Christopher Wren and the other natural philosophers nodded agreement.

Sir Robert Moray asked to speak. As a Scotsman he'd been one of Charles II staunchest friends. He lived at Whitehall and received great favor in the King's court. Sir Robert Moray said, "We can guarantee the invisible college's continued existence by gaining his Majesty's support. We should strive for a Royal charter."

"Would King Charles support a scientific society?" Christopher Wren asked.

"Without a doubt," Sir Robert said. "His Majesty is interested in new learning. As you may know, I have a laboratory at Whitehall. His Majesty often comes to the laboratory to talk about natural philosophy with me. He is an amateur astronomer. He has seen through his own great telescope the rings of Saturn and the satellites of Jupiter. He enjoys learning about the marvels of science."

Those present agreed to form a new organization. They drew up a list of forty names. The list included all of the regular members of the invisible college: Robert Boyle, Seth Ward, John Wilkins, Christopher Wren and Henry Oldenburg. They set the membership fee at a shilling a week.

They elected Sir Robert Moray as temporary president. He would try to secure the interest of Charles II.

Henry Oldenburg became the recording secretary of the new organization. He wrote letters to important people in England, asking for their support. He wrote, "We do not restrict our membership to natural philosophers alone. We have peers, bishops, literary men, statesmen, and any others who express curiosity in the new learning. Our members exchange information about the most recent scientific discoveries.''

The new organization grew. Samuel Pepys, the naval department employee who kept the daily diary, became a member.

After months of planning and growth, Sir Robert Moray brought the good news. ''His Majesty has given his blessing. He has granted our petition for a Royal charter. He even asked that we enter his own name as a member. He stated that he would be pleased to receive a private demonstration of our discoveries.''

''What shall we show him?'' Robert Boyle wondered. ''It shouldn't be something merely to raise wonder. Nor should it be tedious or require a prolonged explanation. Mr. Hooke has built a model of the human eye. He can show it and explain how it works. Dr. Clarke has a collection of insects . . .''

Christopher Wren interrupted. ''You are our most important member,'' he said. ''You should present the bulk of the program.''

The humble and courteous Robert Boyle was always surprised at his own fame. At the insistence of his fellow scientists, Robert Boyle presented half

of the twenty demonstrations. He showed how air pressure could hold two polished marble slabs together, even when a weight hung from the lower one. He caused a natural loadstone to lose its magnetism by heating it. He changed the magnetism of a bar magnet by striking it sharply. He performed chemical experiments and also demonstrated the air pump.

Charles II was a tall man, more than six feet tall, and a couple of years younger than Robert Boyle. He seemed perfectly at ease discussing scientific matters. He spoke softly. "Have you selected a name for your organization?" Charles II asked.

"Yes," Robert Boyle said. "We have changed our name from the invisible college to the Royal Society of London for Improving Natural Knowledge. We have even selected a motto: *Nullis in Verba*."

Sir Robert Moray said, "As your Majesty doubtless knows, the words are taken from Horace, and mean roughly, 'Nothing by mere authority.' "

Robert Boyle said, "The motto shows our intention to seek truth by observation and experimentation. We will not accept unproven statements from the works of Aristotle or other ancient authorities."

After King Charles left, everyone agreed that the meeting had gone very well. Not only had King Charles enjoyed the meeting, but so had the regular members. Christopher Wren said, "We need someone to demonstrate new experiments to us the same way we showed our findings to his Majesty."

Robert Boyle agreed. "We can create a post of curator of experiments. The curator's duties will be to show us each week an interesting experiment based upon the latest discoveries of science."

"Who could possibly fill such a post?" Christopher Wren wondered. "It will require a most remarkable individual, someone who knows something about all fields of science."

Robert Boyle said, "Only one person has the special skills and abilities to fill such a post. I'm thinking about Mr. Robert Hooke."

Christopher Wren instantly agreed. "Yes, Mr. Hooke is the right person for the job. But . . . if he comes to London, you will lose his services in Oxford."

Robert Boyle said, "He is the most brilliant assistant I am ever likely to have. I will miss him. However, I shall urge him to accept this position because it will benefit the Royal Society."

Robert Hooke agreed to the new duties, although the Royal Society couldn't pay him a regular salary at first. At each weekly meeting, he showed three or four important demonstrations. He repeated experiments by others and included some of his own devising.

Mr. Hooke's transfer to London forced a difficult decision upon Robert Boyle. Which city—London or Oxford—should he make his permanent home?

Catharine urged him to move to London. "Pall Mall is being improved, along with the park," Catharine said. "This part of London is a pleasant place to live. You could move here and be with your friends."

While Robert wondered about which city to make his home, an important but little noticed event took place in London. In a poorer part of the city, a landlord opened the room occupied by his cleaning woman. He found her body inside. Dark sores covered her skin, clear evidence that she'd died of the Black Death.

Three hundred years earlier that terrible disease had swept across Europe. At first, a city would suffer a few deaths from the plague. Then it would slowly grow worse from one year to the next. Finally, the Black Death would suddenly grip the city, killing as many as one person in four.

Although no one noticed it yet, London had fallen into the same depressing pattern. The Black Death poised, ready to strike.

Robert Boyle knew none of this. "Should I stay in London," he mused. "Or, should I return to Oxford?"

# 11

# A City On Fire

Robert Boyle did return to Oxford. Christopher Wren made the decision easier for him. Christopher Wren resigned his post at Greshem College in London. He accepted a more important position at Oxford University.

Robert Boyle and Christopher Wren teamed with Thomas Willis, a physician, to investigate blood circulation. They carried out a series of experiments to test whether liquids injected into the bloodstream flowed throughout the body.

The experiments began when Chistopher Wren asked, "How does the blood affect the brain? What would happen if we introduced different substances into the blood. Would the blood carry them through the body and into the brain?"

Such an experiment was too dangerous to try on humans. The three scientists selected a dog, a large cross-bred spaniel, for their experiment. Dr. Willis opened a vein in one of the dog's back legs. Robert Boyle filled a hollow quill with opium mixed with wine. Opium is a strong drug. Robert injected the drug into the open vein.

They watched the dog closely. Within moments he stopped struggling against the straps that held him to the table. He breathed shallowly, his mouth hung open and his eyes closed.

Christopher Wren said, ''The drug has already reached his brain.''

Robert Boyle said, ''He is going to sleep.''

"Opium must have greater power when we inject it directly into the blood," Dr. Willis warned. "The opium is killing him."

Robert Boyle began untying the straps. "Quick! Take him to the garden. Keep him moving." Each man took turns running the groggy spaniel back and forth to keep him awake. After a while, the dog recovered.

This experiment showed the role of blood in carrying substances throughout the body. The men carried out other experiments of similar natures. The spaniel became famous. A thief thought he could steal the dog and earn a profit by selling the animal. The dog vanished. Robert Boyle and his friends never saw him again.

When it came time to report their discoveries, the three investigators decided against holding any formal scientific meetings at Oxford.

"There is but one Royal Society," Robert Boyle said. "A rival group would weaken it. The Royal Society meets in London and in that city alone. I shall travel to London whenever possible to attend the weekly meetings."

Christopher Wren grumbled, "The journey from Oxford to London is tedious and time-consuming."

Robert Boyle said, "If you cannot attend in person, you can send papers for Mr. Hooke or Henry Oldenburg to read. They'll keep you informed of important discoveries by other members."

Despite the hazards of cold weather, Robert Boyle preferred traveling to London in winter. The frosty air and cover of snow gave the city a healthier smell and cleaner appearance.

"London is not an attractive city," Robert Boyle said, "especially in summer."

Catharine objected, "Pall Mall is a beautiful place."

Robert Boyle had to agree with her. In summer or winter, this part of London could not be more pleasant. Those who visited Pall Mall walked along a surface of crushed cockleshells. A double row of stately elm trees grew along the street. Fashionable stores operated along Pall Mall. The area became so successful that other store-lined streets tried to capture the feeling of Pall Mall. These storekeepers called their streets shopping malls.

St. James Park and the Royal Gardens bordered on one side of Pall Mall. When Charles II became King, he improved St. James Park. His friends sent him animals from all over the world. He released them in the park, making it an open air zoo. Deer from several countries roamed the grounds, as did guinea-fowl and Arabian sheep. The most famous resident was a pet crane with a wooden leg which a friendly soldier had made for him.

A lake curved through the park. On cold winter days, Robert Boyle and his sister watched groups ice skate on the frozen lake.

"This is a pretty sight," Catharine said.

Robert agreed. "However, the rich have fine brick homes. The poor are not as fortunate. Four hundred thousand people live in London. Most of their dwellings are old, wooden structures, held together by tar and plaster. Garbage, not cockleshells, cover the streets. Rats, not exotic animals, roam the alleys."

While in London, Robert Boyle sat for his first portrait. He bought a fine, flowing wig for the occasion. Doctors, lawyers, and court officials wore long and elaborately curled periwigs. Robert Boyle wore his wig during important state occasions such as meetings with Charles II. Robert showed the portrait to his friends.

Mr. Hooke, in addition to his many other talents, was an excellent artist. He examined the engraving critically. "The face is well done," he pronounced. "It looks just like you."

Robert Boyle said, "I'll use the likeness to illustrate the front pages of my books."

Henry Oldenburg asked, "Is your book about heat and cold ready for the press? I urge you to finish it. Because of the exceptionally cold winter, people have an interest in the subject. The book should sell well." Henry Oldenburg published several of Robert's scientific books. Robert signed the profits over to him. It was a dignified way to pay Henry Oldenburg for his services.

Robert had already begun a series of experiments on heat and cold. At first, the lack of an accurate thermometer held him back. To investigate heat properly he needed an instrument that measured temperature accurately.

Galileo had invented a crude air thermometer in 1597. Galileo took a glass bulb with a long stem. He heated the bulb, driving out some of the air. He turned it upside down with the long stem in a container of colored water.

When the temperature fell, this cooled the air, causing it to contract. The reduced air pressure allowed water to rise part way up the long stem. When the temperature rose, this heated the air, causing it to expand. The greater air pressure drove some of the water from the stem.

Robert quickly learned that changes in air pressure also caused the colored water to rise and fall. Worst of all, in cold weather, the water in the tube froze, making the air thermometer useless.

Robert Boyle replaced the colored water with colored alcohol. Alcohol didn't freeze in winter. He sealed the thermometer. This did away with changes caused by air pressure. He could carry the sealed thermometer about without spilling the colored alcohol. Robert Boyle improved upon Galileo's design to such an extent it became a serious scientific instrument.

Other scientists, as well as ordinary citizens, asked for copies of the thermometer. Robert Boyle set his glassblowers to work. Soon small, alcohol thermometers became common in England. Robert Boyle put his thermometer to practical use. He mounted one outside his door. He consulted it before leaving home. He chose a light or heavy cloak depending upon the temperature.

To conduct experiments regarding the cold, he at first waited for cold weather. Then he discovered he could lower the temperature far below freezing by mixing salt with crushed ice. Containers of water set in such a mixture froze quickly.

People had long noticed that closed containers of water cracked when the water froze. Robert made a quick test of the power of freezing water. He selected a gun barrel with a thick steel wall. He filled the barrel with water and tightly closed each end with screws. He buried the gun barrel in a mixture of ice and salt. After two hours he pulled it out and brushed off the ice. The water had frozen inside the gun barrel and cracked it.

What caused the ice to split the gun barrel? Scientists offered two possible explanations. One group explained it this way: "All substances expand when heated and contract when cooled. When water changes to ice, the contraction leaves a vacuum. The sides of the gun barrel crack to allow air inside to fill the vacuum."

The other group explained the split gun barrel this way: "Most substances do contract as they cool. However, water is an exception. It expands as it freezes. The enormous expansive force of ice causes the gun barrel to split.''

Robert Boyle believed the second explanation to be the true one. How could he prove it? This time he used a glass jar rather than a gun barrel. He half filled the jar with water and partially buried it in a pail filled with crushed ice and salt water. Then he added ice alone to the pail. This arrangement put the colder temperature at the bottom of the jar. The water froze from the bottom up, forcing the water higher in the jar. Finally, the entire contents of the glass container froze. This proved that water is not like most other liquids. It *expands* as it turns to a solid.

Robert Boyle found that ice occupies about nine percent more space than the water from which it forms. Ice is lighter than water, which explains why it floats in water.

Robert Boyle also investigated heat and cold with the air pump. He placed a small container of warm water in the receiver of the air pump. He sealed the receiver and began pumping out the air. The lukewarm water began to boil! The reduced air pressure let the warm water boil at a lower than normal temperature. Robert Boyle concluded that water on a high mountain would boil at a lower temperature than at sea level.

Robert Boyle continued to visit London. At the June 7, 1665, weekly meeting of the Royal Society, Samuel Pepys reported a disturbing sight. He came in, his face lined with concern.

"What is the matter?" Robert Boyle asked.

"I saw three red crosses on the doors of houses along Drury Lane," Samuel Pepys said. "The Black Death has struck those houses."

"Hot weather always brings a few cases of the Black Death," Mr. Hooke said.

"Never so early in the year," Samuel Pepys said. "The Black Death is growing in London. I fear we are in for an epidemic." He shuddered at the thought.

"What causes it?" Robert Boyle asked.

Christopher Wren said, "No one knows. Some say it is caused by bad air. Others think it is caused by overcrowding. Others blame the filth in the streets."

"What can we do to keep it from spreading?" Robert Boyle asked.

Samuel Pepys said, "The best anyone can do is close a house where sickness has occurred. Paint a cross on the door. Set a guard on the house. Keep the victims inside and hope the disease will not spread."

"What should we do?" Robert Boyle wondered.

Christopher Wren said, "The safest course of action is to leave the city. I've never traveled abroad. For a long time I've wanted to visit Paris. I shall make plans to do so if the plague becomes worse."

The plague did become worse—much worse. By the end of July an appalling outburst of the Black Death gripped the city. Ten thousand people died in that month alone. It showed no signs of letting up.

In a panic wealthy men sent wives and children away to their country estates. The men stayed behind only long enough to close their businesses and lock their doors. Then they fled, too. Officials closed Greshem College. The Royal Society canceled its meetings. The members scattered. Robert Boyle returned to Oxford. Christopher Wren left for Paris.

Only two members of the Royal Society bravely stayed behind—Samuel Pepys and Henry Oldenburg.

Henry Oldenburg wrote to the other Royal Society members. He kept them informed of the terrible conditions in London. "Business has ground to a halt. Parts of the city are deserted. The weekly lists of the dead make grim reading. At this rate the Black Death will carry away eighty thousand people before winter.''

A few days later, Robert Boyle received a message from his sister. She'd moved to Mary's home in Leeze. ''Everyone here is in good health,'' she reported. She warned her brother that he should expect Royal visitors at Oxford. ''The King and Court are leaving London. They will seek safety by moving to Oxford.''

Robert Boyle despaired of conducting experiments while the Court stayed in Oxford. Charles II demanded the attendance of the great Robert Boyle at court events. Royal visitors interrupted his experiments at home.

Catharine urged him to come to Leeze and stay at Mary's house. Robert looked into the offer but decided against it. Mary had opened her house to members of the Boyle family who fled London. Aunts, uncles, nieces and nephews made Mary's house their home. They overran the place. Living with her would hardly be better than staying in Oxford.

Once again he called upon Henry Oldenburg. His puritan friend found temporary lodging for him at Newington, an isolated village a few miles outside London. Henry Oldenburg walked out to the village. The two friends inspected the house and grounds.

''Behind the building is a large orchard. It will be a good place to walk and meditate,'' Henry Oldenburg said.

Robert Boyle said, ''I imagine the air is considerably better than in London.''

Henry Oldenburg agreed. ''The smell of death and rotting garbage is everywhere,'' he said. ''To walk the streets I must pick my way through the filth. Some people plug their noses with wormwood and breathe through their mouths. Others hold handkerchiefs scented with herbs to their faces.''

Robert Boyle said, ''I'll live here until the Black Death runs its course. Then I'll relocate in London. But what of you my friend? Aren't you concerned you'll fall victim to the Black Death?''

Henry Oldenburg said, ''Despite the danger, my chief concern is the papers of the Royal Society. What would happen to them if the Lord should visit me?''

Poor Henry Oldenburg, Robert Boyle thought. He fears less for his life than for losing the papers put in his trust. ''What have you done to protect the papers?'' Robert Boyle asked.

''The best I can do,'' Henry Oldenburg said, ''is leave written instructions about what to do with them should I succumb to the plague. I've separated them into bundles—your book manuscripts, the Royal Society's scientific papers, and my own correspondence. I've sealed the bundles and listed their contents on the outside. If I should fall ill, I'll send the bundles to a safe place.''

By the end of August, 1666, the worst of the Black Death appeared to be over. Cautiously, the survivors living in the country returned to their homes. They believed another disaster as bad as the Black Death would not befall the city anytime soon. They were wrong.

On September 1, 1666, just before midnight, Thomas Farynor, the King's baker went to bed in his house on Pudding Lane. Downstairs he'd piled brushwood to heat the bread ovens. Sometime in the early hours of Sunday morning, a spark flew from the kitchen hearth. It set the wood afire.

Thomas Farynor awoke to the sound of flames roaring up the stairs. He roused the other three members

of his household. They scrambled to the roof. Thomas, his daughter and one maid jumped to safety on the roof next door. Another maid acted too slowly. She died when the roof collapsed into the burning building.

A steady wind drove the fire from one house to the next along Pudding Lane toward the Thames River.

The city night watch summoned Sir Thomas Bludworth, the mayor of London. He arrived on the scene at three in the morning. The mayor failed to take decisive action. "You should not have disturbed me from my sleep," he said. "The fire will burn itself out when it reaches the river."

Robert Boyle saw the fire, too. Catharine had moved back to Pall Mall. Robert Boyle, who'd suffered ill health during the summer, came to stay with her for a while. One of Catharine's maids awakened them to report the fire. Robert arose and walked in his nightclothes to the window. Because of the distance, he thought it a minor fire. Like so many other people, he went back to sleep, thinking it would all be over in the morning.

The next morning began the worst four days in the city's history. The fire reached the Thames. All along the river, warehouses held casks of oil, barrels of pitch and tar, and stacks of lumber. Piles of coal had been unloaded from barges. All of this burned furiously. Rather than going out when it reached the Thames River, the flame flared into a gigantic firestorm.

The flames raced up and down the river banks, and leaped the narrow streets, setting rows of buildings afire. The cobblestones glowed red hot. They cracked with a sound as loud as rifle shots. The fire burned out of control.

City leaders tried to contain it by making fire lanes. They pulled down buildings with great iron grappling hooks. When this failed, they used gunpowder to blast wider paths. This, and a shift in the winds, ended the four days of chaos. The fire died out, but not before it wiped out a square mile of the city.

Robert Boyle, Henry Oldenburg and Christopher Wren walked through the blackened city. Christopher Wren summarized the extent of the disaster. "It was the worst fire in the city's history," he said. "Three-fourths of London is in ruins. The fire destroyed ten thousand homes and ninety of the city churches, including Old St. Paul's. Everyone thought St. Paul's would be spared. But look at it now."

Henry Oldenburg surveyed the ruins glumly. "Alas for my carefully preserved papers. When the fire threatened my home, I carried them here thinking it would be safe."

"All of them are lost?" Robert Boyle asked.

"Yes," Henry Oldenburg said. "Your book manuscripts, the transactions of the Royal Society, and my private letters. All of them are destroyed."

Henry Oldenburg was not alone. When the fire began, neighborhood booksellers believed their books would be safe in the basement of the huge stone building. They carried books valued at 150,000 pounds to the basement.

The roof of the old building was made of timber covered by a skin of lead. On the third day of the fire, the roof timbers caught fire, and the roof crashed down. The heat melted the lead, which ran down into the basement. The intense heat of the molten lead set the precious storehouse of books afire.

The rubble of old St. Paul's still smoldered. Robert Boyle walked closer. "Ouch!" he said and stepped back. "The cobblestones are still hot. It even burned my feet through the soles of my shoes."

A sudden gust of wind blew across the ruins, stirring

up charred paper. Henry Oldenburg grasped at the flying paper. He caught a piece. "It's part of a book," he said.

Christopher Wren said, "The building itself is no great loss. It has been in a deplorable state for years. This merely saves the expense of trying to repair it. Now we can build a new and improved St. Paul's."

A few days later, city leaders put Christopher Wren in charge of rebuilding not only St. Paul's, but the rest of the city as well. He reported to the Royal Society about his plans. "I will lay out wider streets, build homes of brick instead of wood. The city will have better churches and more hospitals. We'll dig canals for better drainage. We can keep the city free of rats, filth and stagnant water. It will be a cleaner, healthier place to live." He asked Mr. Hooke to be his chief assistant in redesigning the city.

Robert Boyle took delight in knowing that members of the Royal Society would play such an important role in rebuilding the city. He expected Catharine to share his enthusiasm for the plan for a new London.

Instead, Catharine objected. She thought the grand design would delay reconstruction. "City leaders must restore London as quickly as possible," she said.

Robert disagreed. "This is our best chance to set the city right. It will take time, but it will be worth it."

"Come with me," Catharine said. She took her brother to a field north of town. More than a hundred thousand homeless people camped in the field. They huddled in tents made from blankets and sheets. "These people will be homeless until a new London can grow up from the old ruins."

Robert Boyle looked at the astonishing sight. "This is the most remarkable spectacle I have ever beheld," he said. "We must do something for these unfortunate people."

He and his strong-willed sister contributed their money and time to aid the victims of the Great Fire.

Despite the hardships, the citizens of London endured the delays. They believed it would mean a better city, one in which the Black Death might never return.

Once again the Royal Society began holding regular Wednesday afternoon meetings. They shared Gresham College with the city government, which had taken over the building after the Great Fire. With everything nearly back to normal, the meeting looked like a family reunion. As the members arrived, they shook hands and exchanged stories about how they'd survived the Black Death and Great Fire.

Lord Brouncker, president of the Royal Society, came to whisper a question in Robert's ear. "It is time to bring the meeting to order, but Mr. Oldenburg is not yet here. Should we begin the meeting without our secretary?"

"Henry Oldenburg is always prompt," Robert Boyle said. "His absence puzzles me."

Suddenly Samuel Pepys burst into the assembly. He cried, "Henry Oldenburg has been arrested as a spy!"

# 12

# The Skeptical Chemist

The news of Henry Oldenburg's arrest shocked the members of the Royal Society. The government had clamped him in the Tower, London's prison for religious and political prisoners.

"Our secretary in jail?" Robert Boyle asked. "I don't believe it. What charge could the government possibly bring against Henry Oldenburg?"

Christopher Wren waved a hand toward the members of the Royal Society. He said, "We do not allow religious or political differences to keep us from exchanging views on scientific matters. The government is not as tolerant. Henry Oldenburg is a Puritan at a time when the Puritans have lost their political power. His religious beliefs could be the reason behind his arrest."

"Or perhaps it's because he's a German by birth," Lord Brouncker said. "Any government becomes suspicious of foreigners when there have been disasters such as the Black Death and Great Fire.''

Samuel Pepys said, ''But the government hasn't formally charged him yet, but they suspect him. He writes letters and sends them all over the world. They'll use his letter writing as evidence against him.''

Robert Boyle said, ''I'm confident he will prove to be an innocent person.''

Once again, Robert Boyle did his best for a friend in trouble. He and others in the Royal Society worked to have the charges dropped before Henry Oldenburg's trial began.

Two months passed. Despite their best efforts, Henry Oldenburg stayed locked in the Tower. Robert Boyle shook his head, exasperated. ''Henry survived the Black Death and Great Fire only to lose his freedom because he writes letters! We must make the officials understand that it is his profession to spread scientific learning.''

Finally, after three months, the innocent man walked free. As soon as his guards released him, Henry Oldenburg came to Pall Mall to thank Robert Boyle.

''God Almighty bless you,'' Henry Oldenburg said with heart-felt thanks. ''I learned in my confinement to know my real friends. You have all of my gratitude. You cannot ask anything of me that I would not cheerfully obey to the best of my power.''

''What will you do now?'' Robert Boyle asked. ''Will you stay in London? The Royal Society needs you.''

''The air in the prison stifled me,'' Henry Oldenburg said. ''As soon as my release from the Tower, I promised myself to walk into the country. I will spend some days in the good air of Crawford in Kent. Once I breathe fresh air for a while I shall return.''

After the release of Henry Oldenburg, Robert Boyle

ended his stay in Oxford. He decided to live in London with his sister. Robert Boyle left Oxford in the fall of 1668. He transferred his home, laboratory, library, assistants and secretaries to the house in Pall Mall.

Twenty-four years earlier he'd landed in England after his travels in Europe. Alone and penniless he'd walked the streets of London, unsure of what to do. There by chance he'd met Catharine. She'd taken him into her home. Now, after all these years, he once again called Catharine's house his home.

Catharine instructed Thomas, her butler, to give Robert whatever help he needed. Thomas set up the laboratory and housed Robert's staff of assistants. He unpacked and shelved Robert's personal library of three thousand books.

Pall Mall houses had not been built for scientific research. Robert supervised installing the chemical furnace in a back room. Somehow he found floor space for all of the glasses, pots, retorts, pumps, receivers, chemical bottles and bundles of research papers. He even crowded some of it into his bed chamber, leaving only enough room for a few chairs.

A next-door neighbor, Isaac Barrow paid Robert a visit. Isaac Barrow had been one of the original members of the invisible college. He was an able mathematician and preacher of the gospel. Isaac Barrow was very strong, with the courage to match, although he was rather small in size. He had a lean figure, calm assurance and clear grey eyes. He'd left Cambridge's Trinity College to become the personal chaplain of King Charles.

"One of the reasons I stepped aside in Cambridge," Isaac Barrow said, "was to give my post to a young genius named Isaac Newton. You'll hear more about him. But tell me why you left Oxford after so many productive years?"

"Oxford has been good to me," Robert Boyle agreed. "The university honored me with the degree of Doctor of Physics. It's the only academic degree I've ever received. However, the center of scientific learning has shifted to London. My place is here with the Royal Society."

Robert Boyle didn't mention another important reason to come to London—his health. For years, he had suffered from a variety of ailments, including painful kidney stones and malaria. Once, while at Stalbridge he became too weak to leave his bed. Servants carried him by litter to the resort town of Bath. He resolved not to leave until he could ride away on his own horse. Although he recovered, he never again enjoyed the best of health.

Catharine insisted that he come to London. "I'll be here to help you when you become too ill to care for yourself," she said.

Robert Boyle also suffered from weak eyes. This condition made it difficult for him to read by candlelight. He employed assistants to read to him after dark and to take his dictation.

"I can't entirely avoid reading at night," Robert Boyle confessed to his sister. "The reading assistants do help. I dictate only the first draft. After they copy it down, I read through the manuscript and make corrections." Robert Boyle had high standards for his books. He would not publish them without a careful proofreading.

His eyes continued to trouble him, although they grew no worse.

Robert Boyle pressed ahead despite the pain and physical ailments. His mind remained sharp and eager to attack the problems of science. Under Catharine's watchful care, Robert Boyle spent long hours in his laboratory at the back of the London house.

In London he continued his studies of heat. What part does air play in combustion, Robert Boyle wondered. Is air necessary for a fire to burn?

Anytime a substance is burned in a closed container, it eventually goes out. How did most scientists explain this observation? They said that fumes from the fire filled the container and smothered the flame. Robert had proved that a candle flame needs air, or at least something in the air, to keep it burning.

Robert decided it would be better first to put the substance to be tested in the receiver and then to set it afire. He borrowed a large burning glass from the Royal Society. The burning glass started a fire by bringing the rays of the sun to a focus.

He placed paper in a sealed receiver and focused the sun's rays on it through the glass wall of the receiver. With air in the receiver, the paper burned briskly for a few moments before dying out. Without air in the receiver, the paper wouldn't ignite.

The burning glass wasn't entirely satisfactory. The thick glass wall of the receiver scattered the sun's rays. The focused rays only got hot enough to ignite substances that burned easily, like paper. Besides, Robert could only experiment at midday during bright, sunny weather.

Robert found a better solution. He heated a metal plate until it glowed red hot. He placed the red hot plate at the bottom of the receiver. He loosely attached the test material to a wire hanging over the hot plate. After sealing the receiver, he shook the wire, causing the material to fall to the hot plate.

With this new arrangement he tested sulfur, a yellow chemical used in the manufacture of gunpowder. He dropped it on the hot plate with air in the receiver. The sulfur burned with a sputtering, blue flame. He dropped it on the hot plate with the air removed from the receiver. The sulfur melted and fumed, but it did not burn.

Mr. Hooke heard of Robert Boyle's experiments. He said, "Have you tried gunpowder? I've concluded from my research that it does not need air to burn." Gunpowder is an explosive mixture of saltpeter, charcoal and sulfur.

Robert Boyle tested Mr. Hooke's statement. In a receiver filled with air, the gunpowder exploded in a flash when it hit the hot plate. In a receiver empty of air, the gunpowder didn't explode, but it did burn briskly.

Robert sat back, puzzled by these observations. If gunpowder would burn in a vacuum, then it should also burn under water. He packed a goose quill with gunpowder. He lit the end and quickly plunged it under water. Dark bubbles filled with smoke boiled to the surface. He watched in amazement. A steady red flame flickered under water. Gunpowder did burn under water!

Mr. Hooke said, "Gunpowder burns in a vacuum and under water because it contains a substance that is also present in air."

Robert Boyle warned, "Let's not be too hasty to draw that conclusion. Air might be trapped in the pores of water or between the grains of gunpowder. We cannot be absolutely certain that the combustion occurred without air."

Mr. Hooke said, "You are entirely too cautious about drawing a conclusion."

"I'd rather be cautious than come to a conclusion that later turns out to be false," Robert Boyle said.

He next turned to the study of respiration, or breathing. Suppose a small animal like a mouse or bird is placed in a receiver and the air pumped out. The animal would be frisky at first. As the air was removed, it would pant and drop its head. Finally, if the experiment were not stopped in time, the animal would die. The poor animal's slow death struck Robert as similar to the smothering of a candle flame in the vacuum receiver.

"I am impressed by the similarity between respiration and combustion," he reported to the Royal Society. "A living animal needs a constant supply of air to keep alive. A candle flame needs a constant supply of air to burn brightly. I venture to suggest that a part of the air is necessary for life, and that breathing and burning are essentially the same."

One member of the Royal Society said, "Most scientists think the purpose of breathing is to carry away vapor from the lungs."

Robert Boyle agreed in part with that view. "Breathing does remove waste products from the blood," he said. "However, there seems to be more to breathing than merely exhaling vapor. I suspect that the air does something else in respiration, which we cannot yet explain."

It bothered some scientists when they didn't have all the answers. On the other hand, Robert Boyle readily admitted that many of his discoveries needed further study.

He said, "The book of nature is a fine and large piece of tapestry rolled up, which we are not able to see all at once. We must be content to wait for the discovery of its beauty and symmetry. Little by little it will gradually come to be more and more unfolded."

Shortly after Robert moved to Pall Mall, a messenger delivered a package to the house. Catharine unwrapped the parcel. "It's a book from John Milton," she said. "He's written a note of appreciation inside the cover. He thanks us for standing behind him during the restoration." The blind poet gave Robert and Catharine an autographed copy of his latest book, *Paradise Lost*.

Charles II had not forgotten Robert Boyle either. He still owed Robert a favor. Charles II received a grant of land in Ireland. Without any advance warning, he turned the land over to Robert Boyle.

"What will you do with your surprise gift?" his sister asked.

Robert thought about the matter. "It's a real puzzle," he admitted. "I have enough income of my own. I'll use the money for Christian works."

His sister knew that Robert Boyle's natural humility led him to do many good works in secret. For years he provided relief to the poor in Ireland, just as he'd worked behind the scenes to help the victims of the

Great Fire. He'd also given great sums of money to hard-working, poor preachers and their wives and children. He did this so quietly that the people he helped often never learned his name.

Suddenly Robert remembered the need for a Bible in the Irish language. "I'll set aside part of the money for translating and printing a Bible in Gaelic."

"What about the rest?" his sister asked.

"I'll use the remainder for spreading the gospel in New England and for missionary efforts to the American Indians," Robert decided.

Robert spent two-thirds of the land grant money for the Irish Bible. He hired Dr. Andrew Sall of Christ Church, Oxford, for the difficult task of translating the Bible. Once complete, Robert paid for the printing and distribution in Ireland. The new Bibles also found their way into Scotland, for that country needed a Gaelic Bible, too.

As time passed, Robert Boyle ordered the translation of Scriptures into other languages as well. He had five hundred copies of the four Gospels and Acts of the Apostles printed for the Malayans. He also paid for the printing of portions of the Bible in Turkish and Arabic.

One day Charles II called Robert Boyle to Whitehall. "I have learned of your missionary efforts," Charles II said. "I wish to appoint you Governor of the Corporation for Propagating the Gospel in New England."

"I shall take the position most seriously," Robert Boyle assured the King. He devoted a lot of time to his new duties. His strict honesty and his shrewd business sense got the most from the Corporation's limited funds. The money went to educate missionaries and to help the natives.

John Eliot, a missionary to the American Indians,

wrote to Robert Boyle. "Your charity toward the poor natives of New England is greater than from any other source."

Some people looked down on the Indians as an inferior race. Robert Boyle seldom became angry. But prejudice and injustice would cause a flash of anger and distress to cross his face. He gave freely to those in need, without thought of race or nationality. He pointed out that all people are members of the human race.

When Charles II asked for a report on the missionary activities, Robert could say, "The work is going well. Leaders of the American Colonies keep me informed of the latest news from the New World, both religious and scientific. William Penn of the Quaker Colony has written letters describing the Indians and his dealings with them. Governor John Winthrop of Connecticut wrote me about a mysterious death of fish in a pond. The Indians think it is due to lightning striking the pond."

Charles II said, "Your success as Governor of the Corporation has brought your name to the attention of the East India Company."

The East India Company had been formed almost eighty years earlier by a group of London merchants. The company traded with India and the islands in the Indian Ocean. The company made fabulous sums of money from the trade in spices, silk, and precious gems.

Charles II said, "I can offer you an appointment to the board of directors of the company."

Robert Boyle accepted the offer. His friends wondered why he joined the company. It had nothing to do with either science or religion. They learned his motive at the next meeting of the board of directors.

When it came time for him to speak, Robert Boyle

said, "I venture to make a motion. We should give thought to do something for spreading the gospel to the natives of the Orient."

One of the other directors objected. "We are merchants, not missionaries."

Robert Boyle said, "We are Christians. God has blessed our enterprise. The East India Company must become more than a business venture. We take great wealth from the Orient. We should attempt to improve the state of the people in those countries."

Robert managed to persuade his business associates to help spread Christianity in the countries where their ships landed. In addition, company ships began carrying scientists. These naturalists studied the weather, the seas and other interesting scientific sights during the long sea voyages. When the ships anchored for water and food, naturalists rowed ashore to explore. They collected unusual plants and animals to bring back to England for detailed study. Both religion and science benefited when Robert Boyle became a director of the East India Company.

Robert's many activities were suddenly interrupted two years after he moved to Pall Mall. He suffered a stroke that completely paralyzed him. He was not able to move, or bring his hand to his mouth.

The terrible tragedy left Robert Boyle with a mind as sharp as ever, but a body that couldn't move. He couldn't even speak.

# 13

# The Christian Gentleman

The stroke left Robert Boyle paralyzed and in danger of death. After a week his doctor took him off the danger list, but the stroke left him almost helpless. He could not read or write or move from his bed.

The friends of Robert Boyle shook their heads in sadness because of the great tragedy. For most victims, such attacks would signal the end of their active lives. Robert's friends assumed his scientific career to be over.

But Robert Boyle was far from finished with life. His body might not be fully working, but there was nothing wrong with his mind. The stroke could not prevent him from thinking about scientific problems.

Slowly he improved. On good days, he could speak, but only by carefully forming each word. His assistants read to him and took dictation. He described experiments for them to carry out. Robert did some of his most important work while confined to his bed.

The months passed. Robert Boyle learned to ignore his tired body, weak eyes and attacks of fevers, chills and kidney stones. After eleven months, he gathered his strength and left his bed for the first time.

His comeback amazed his friends. What could explain his near miraculous recovery? Certainly death did not frighten Robert Boyle. As a Christian he looked forward to the resurrection. He believed the promise of a home in heaven for those who served the Lord. He also believed spiritual strength could overcome physical limitations. His God-given patience and gritty determination helped him get better.

Although Robert Boyle never fully recovered, he did go on to even greater scientific feats. During the five years *after* the stroke, he made more discoveries and wrote more books than in the five years *before* the stroke.

Robert Boyle achieved world-wide renown as a scientist and as a spokesman for Christian causes. Visitors besieged him as soon as he was well enough to receive company. Friends and relatives made an appearance to wish him well. Missionaries came to discuss the problems of spreading the gospel. Church leaders sought his help in fighting religious injustice. Scientists visited his laboratory to learn more about his scientific methods.

Many others knocked at his door simply to be able to say they'd met the great Robert Boyle. The idle curious hoped he would admit them to his laboratory to see some new discovery.

Robert Boyle did not disappoint them. Doctors, lawyers, noblemen, fashionable ladies and ordinary tourists visited him. Thomas, the butler, would answer the door and take them to Robert's laboratory. To their delight, Robert showed them amusing and interesting experiments. They examined an improved version of the air pump. They listened as he explained chemical experiments in progress. They stepped back from the heat when he opened the door of his chemical furnace. They ate fish whose bones had been turned to jelly by cooking in Robert's latest invention—a pressure cooker.

Catharine became concerned at the stream of visitors from all over the world. She feared the commotion would strain her brother's delicate health. Catharine said, "You cannot do your duties and marshal your strength if you welcome all who come to our door."

Robert found a solution to the problem. He rented a private lodging in another part of the city. He kept its location concealed from everyone but Catharine. When people pressed upon him and demanded too much of his time, Robert escaped to his secret apartment.

One person Robert Boyle did welcome at Pall Mall was Isaac Newton, the young mathematician from Cambridge. Isaac had a high forehead, square chin, and piercing eyes that grew intent when he thought upon a difficult problem. Although still a young man, his hair had turned completely white.

"Welcome to London," Robert Boyle said. "I am pleased you have found time to visit your friends here."

Isaac Newton studied Robert Boyle. He saw a tall, slender man, one who spoke in a calm, precise voice. Isaac Newton said, "My visit to London is not entirely social. The authorities at Cambridge intend to dismiss me from my teaching post."

"Whatever for?" Robert Boyle asked. "You are Trinity College's best-known instructor."

Isaac Newton explained, "To keep the post I must sign a list of thirty-nine articles of faith. Some of the

articles are in error. To sign the paper would conflict
with my Christian beliefs."

"What can you do?" Robert Boyle asked.

"Only the direct action of His Majesty will keep
me at Cambridge," Isaac Newton said. "One purpose of my visit is to enlist your support when my case
comes before King Charles."

"I shall be happy to help you," Robert Boyle
assured the young scientist.

Robert Boyle took Isaac Newton to meet
Christopher Wren. They rode in a carriage along the
Strand to Luggate Hill. They stopped at the burned-
out remains of old St. Paul's.

Robert Boyle said, "Christopher Wren designed
fifty-one new parish churches. He has finished them
and now turns his efforts to the new St. Paul's. The
Great Fire damaged the old building beyond repair.
It is being pulled down to make way for the new one."

Workmen used a battering ram to knock down a
wall of the old building. It collapsed with a roar and
a cloud of white dust.

Christopher Wren walked over to the carriage. He
shook Isaac Newton's hand and welcomed him to
London.

Isaac said, "I have heard of your model of the new
church."

"Come with me," Christopher Wren said, "I'll
show it to you." He took his visitors to his office at
Whitehall to see the model of the new church. A person could walk into the enormous wooden model and
look around.

Christopher Wren pointed to the great dome.
"Designing the enormous dome was a fascinating
mathematical exercise. Construction of the actual
building is going to be even more challenging. The
Portland quarries can only produce blocks of stone
less than four feet in diameter."

Isaac Newton said, "The building is like nothing I've seen!"

Christopher Wren said, "Church buildings today have to be different from those of the past. Churchgoers of years past played little part in the service, except to sit and listen. Churches conducted their services in Latin, which only a few educated people understood anyway. Churchgoers today expect to join in the worship. The building must be more open so worshipers can see the pulpit from any pew in the building."

Isaac Newton asked, "When will you finish St. Paul's?"

Christopher Wren said, "I've only begun. Its construction will take about thirty-five years. Perhaps I'll see the end of it, although its unlikely. No one who has undertaken the building of a cathedral has lived to see it completed."

On February 18, 1675, Isaac Newton attended his first meeting of the Royal Society. The men pressed forward to greet him: Henry Oldenburg, the solid German; Samuel Pepys, the Naval secretary; and even the bad-tempered Robert Hooke.

Isaac Newton spent six weeks in London. He made the rounds to meet important people who could help him in his cause. Between appointments, he often came to Robert Boyle's home. The two men spent most of their time in Robert's chemistry laboratory. Glasses, pots and chemical instruments crowded the room. Books overflowed from shelves and bundles of paper tumbled from the tables. There was hardly room to sit.

Isaac Newton noticed stains on the floor and strange smells in the air. "Many people talk about the experimental method," Isaac Newton said. "I see that you follow it."

"The scientific method has many critics," Robert Boyle said. "Some university professors resent the Royal Society because we urge them to replace their old-fashioned studies with more modern ones. Some religious leaders level another objection, which disturbs me even more. They charge that the new science encourages a person to doubt the existence of God. They believe that learning more about nature weakens a person's Christian beliefs."

"I have heard the same objections," Isaac Newton said, "but science reveals a purpose behind the grand design of the universe. I've never understood why our opponents regard as atheistic a study which for me merely confirms the great truths of the Bible.''

Robert Boyle knew that Isaac Newton had a fundamental belief in the Bible as the Word of God. Robert Boyle said, ''The more I understand the wonders of nature, the more I am led to admire the wonder of its Creator. The marvelous design of even the simplest living creature is evidence of the existence of God.''

Isaac Newton agreed. ''Atheism is so senseless,'' he said. ''Look at the solar system. The earth is at the right distance from the sun to receive the proper amounts of heat and light. This did not happen by chance.''

Both men believed that God created the universe from the beginning. His creation had a design that they could trace out by experimental science.

Robert Boyle said, ''Nevertheless, if one must choose between becoming a Christian and becoming a scientist, I would rather have more Christians than more scientists. Science can so easily bewitch one and occupy one's time. Often, I must apologize to my sister because chemistry takes so much time from my theological studies.''

''What are you working on now?'' Newton asked.

Robert Boyle said, ''I have begun a series of chemical experiments. My goal is to publish an improved edition of *The Skeptical Chemist*.''

Robert Boyle first published *The Skeptical Chemist* in 1661. A skeptic is a person who questions generally held beliefs. Ancient chemists based their study upon a few simple assumptions. They called these assumptions postulates, or first truths. They believed the postulates to be so obviously true that anyone would accept them without question. Until Robert Boyle's day, most scientists checked whether the conclusions followed logically from the assumptions. In

*The Skeptical Chemist*, Robert Boyle challenged not only the conclusions, but also the basic assumptions of chemistry.

Chief of these assumptions was the four-element theory. The four-element theory of matter assumed that all substances were made of some combination of fire, water, air and earth. Robert Boyle considered the great range of chemical substances: liquids like vinegar and alcohol; solids like sulfur and charcoal; and gases like steam and other vapors. Could only four elements account for the nearly limitless variety of substances in nature?

Robert Boyle's experiments uncovered serious flaws in the four-element theory. Take fire for example. Some of the ancient writers taught that alcohol was made entirely of the fire element because it would burn without leaving a residue. Others taught that alcohol was made entirely of the water element because it was clear and wet like water.

In addition, fire was supposed to separate a substance into simpler ingredients. Yet fire could not separate gold from silver in an alloy of the two metals. On the other hand, *aqua regia*, a strong acid, could separate gold from an alloy of gold and silver.

Robert heated wood under two different conditions, in an open container and in a closed container. In the first case, the wood burned to give ash and soot. In the second case, the wood gave oil, charcoal and three other ingredients. Fire gave two ingredients the first way and five the second way.

Finally, fire didn't always yield simpler substances. Robert mixed sand, limestone and soda ash together. When he heated the mixture, they formed glass. The new compound was more complex than the original. Upon heating, the glass melted, but it didn't separate into the original ingredients of sand, limestone and soda ash.

Robert Boyle urged chemists to abandon the old system. He advised them to build a fresh one based upon experiments. In the first edition of *The Skeptical Chemist*, Robert Boyle replaced alchemy, the false science with chemistry, the true science. The book, like most of his others, received an enthusiastic reception. Despite its success, Robert believed much still needed to be done.

Robert Boyle told Isaac Newton, "I have never been completely satisfied with the book, especially the section about the definition of a chemical element. In the first edition of the book, I destroyed the old four-element theory. In the second edition, I will introduce my own system to replace it."

Isaac Newton encouraged Robert Boyle. "For me, chemistry is far more difficult than mathematics. Years ago, I converted one of my rooms at Trinity into a chemistry laboratory. I have given it my best efforts, but I have discovered nothing I would want to announce with certainty."

Isaac Newton's case came before Charles II on March 12, 1675. His Majesty handed down his decision. He granted Isaac Newton's petition. Isaac could return to Trinity and to his teaching post. He would not be forced to sign the articles of faith.

Robert Boyle continued his efforts to put chemistry on a firm footing. He took the most important step in chemistry. He gave the modern definition of an element.

An *element*, he wrote, is a substance that cannot be separated into simpler substances by chemical means, nor can two or more substances be chemically combined to give an element. In other words, an element is the simplest substance possible, one unmingled with anything else.

He offered an example to make this definition easier to understand. Gold, he suggested, might be an element, since countless experiments had failed to alter it in any way. A chemist cannot make gold by combining it with other metals. Nor can a chemist separate gold into two or more different substances.

Chemists would discover true elements only by constantly seeking them. Slowly the list of elements grew: gold, silver, copper, tin, zinc, iron, lead, mercury, sulfur, carbon, phosphorus, oxygen and nitrogen. Eventually, chemists would identify more than a hundred elements.

Robert Boyle's definition of an element made the second edition of *The Skeptical Chemist* the most important book on chemistry ever published.

In 1680, the members of the Royal Society elected Robert Boyle president of that organization. Unfortunately, to take office he would have to sign an oath agreeing to several points of religious faith. Like Isaac Newton, he could not attest to religious convictions that differed, however slightly, from those he actually held.

Robert asked Mr. Hooke to thank the Royal Society, but "My conscience is tender when it comes to religious tests. Please ask them to proceed to a new election for I shall not take office."

The Royal Society elected Samual Pepys to the office.

A constant stream of visitors and guests still knocked at Robert's door. Visitors knew they would receive a warm welcome at his home. Because of his frail health, Robert could no longer escape to his secret apartment.

Catharine insisted that he restrict the number of people he saw. "They interfere with your work and leave you exhausted. You must preserve your time and energy.

Robert said, "Some have traveled so far to see me. I don't want to disappoint them by turning them away."

"Then post visiting hours," Catharine said. "Let them know you'll receive guests only on certain days of the week."

At first, Robert rejected Catharine's unusual idea. "People would think it presumptuous of me to post visiting hours as if our home were a museum or the restored residence of some important historical character.''

Eventually, Robert took his sister's wise advice. He published an announcement in the London newspapers. The announcement said, ''Mr. Boyle finds himself obligated to suggest to his friends who want to do him the honor of visiting him that his physician has strongly advised him not to see quite so many people. He desires to be excused from receiving visits on Tuesday and Friday mornings and on Wednesday and Saturday afternoons.''

In addition, he hung a sign outside his house stating when he would be home to receive visitors. The visiting hours gave some part of every day free for uninterrupted work.

History swept past Robert and his sister in the pleasant house at Pall Mall. William and Mary became King and Queen of England. Ireland suffered through another bloody rebellion. Parliament was dismissed and recalled. A new St. Paul's grew up over the old ruins.

In 1690, Catharine celebrated her seventy-fifth birthday. For fifty years, she'd been one of London's best-known citizens. People addressed her with respect by her title, Lady Ranelagh. To Robert, she remained merely his dear sister Catharine. To Catharine, the great Robert Boyle remained little Robyn, who as a boy had eaten the forbidden plums. Many fond memories lingered in the rooms in the house in Pall Mall.

For years, Robert had not known if he would survive from one day to the next. During the summer of 1691, he once again became seriously ill. He sensed that his life was drawing to a close. He called for his lawyer and dictated his will. In the will he provided for relatives, friends, servants and various charities. He left Stalbridge Manor to Lord Viscount Shannon, sweet Frank, his companion during the adventures in Europe. He left a gold ring and other jewelry to Catharine. He left his best microscope and a powerful loadstone to Mr. Hooke.

In addition, Robert provided enough money for a series of yearly lectures, not on science, but on the Christian religion. The specific purpose of the lectures was for proving the Christian religion against unbelievers.

Two days before Christmas in 1691, Catharine died. The event shocked Robert. He'd assumed he would be the first to go. Heartbroken, he laid her to rest in a burial site inside St. Martins-in-the-Fields church in London.

One week later, on December 30, 1691, Robert Boyle retired for the night. He said his prayers and fell heavily back into bed. Normally, he slept fitfully. Normally, aches and chills kept him awake. On this night, however, he rested comfortably and without pain. He pulled up the covers and sank into the bed's welcome warmth. As Robert drifted off into untroubled sleep, he looked forward to a time when he would know no sorrows, no heartaches and no pains. While he slept, Robert Boyle passed from this world to a better one.

He died.

# 14

# Robert Boyle In Today's World

When Robert Boyle died in 1691, people around the world mourned his loss. He had changed forever the scientific landscape. In addition to his many important discoveries, Robert charted a new course for science, one that is still followed today.

Robert Boyle insisted that the future of science lay in the experimental method. He rejected the common practice of looking up answers in old books. Instead, he demanded that scientific conclusions stand the test of experimental proof. He replaced idle speculation with a solid foundation of careful experiments.

He had no patience with secrecy. He urged scientists to quickly report their discoveries. In this way, one scientist could build on the work of others. Robert Boyle set the example. He published promptly. He described his discoveries in an easy-to-read style, one both accurate and clear.

To help scientists share information, Robert Boyle

and his friends started the Royal Society. It became the first group of scientists to meet regularly. The Royal Society still meets today.

In his book *The Spring of Air* Robert Boyle described his experiments with the air pump. He proved what Galileo had guessed, that all bodies fall at the same speed in a vacuum. He also discovered that sound does not travel in a vacuum.

Robert's experiments hinted at the connection between combustion (burning) and respiration (breathing). Both are chemical reactions that make use of oxygen in the air. The study showed that living things do need air to breathe. Everybody knows this fact today, but they didn't until after Robert's experiments.

The air pump became as important as the microscope and telescope to scientists. It opened many new fields for them to explore: the speed of sound, weather, air pressure, combustion and respiration.

Robert Boyle showed that air can be compressed. Until then, people thought of air as a mysterious substance that didn't follow natural laws. Robert measured the volume of a sample of air at a number of different pressures. He summarized these observations with a simple law. He found that the air's volume changed with pressure in a predictable way. This discovery of the relationship between volume and pressure is known as *Boyle's law*.

Robert Boyle also made great strides in meteorology, the study of the weather. He invented an improved thermometer. He confirmed that the mercury level in a barometer could predict fair or foul weather.

Only one year after his book about air, Robert Boyle published *The Skeptical Chemist*. It is one of the most important chemistry books ever published.

Robert Boyle separated chemistry from medicine. He transformed the false science of alchemy into the true science of chemistry. He struck a fatal blow to the Greek idea of only four elements. Instead, he gave the modern definition of an element. An element is a substance that cannot be broken down into still simpler substances by chemical means.

Robert Boyle proposed that all matter must be made of atoms. He said, "We may conceive that God originally created matter in very small particles that are too small to be seen individually." Robert's atomic theory later proved to be true. An atom is a tiny, solid particle. Each element has atoms that differ from the atoms of other elements. The atoms combine to form molecules and compounds.

Chemical reactions are often difficult to understand. Even a skilled scientist can be confused. For instance, the great Isaac Newton did outstanding work in many fields: astronomy, mathematics, physics and optics. Yet, when he turned to chemistry, he made only minor discoveries. Scientists studied Robert Boyle's book. They learned to put his methods into practice. Only then did they make real progress in chemistry.

*The Skeptical Chemist* earned for him a reputation as one of the founders of modern chemistry.

Robert became the best known scientist of his day. He enjoyed international fame. He is one of the greatest scientists of all time. Whenever a list of great scientists is drawn up, Robert Boyle is always listed in the top ten.

Yet, Robert Boyle never considered science his chief concern. He was a devout Christian and Bible scholar. He always put his service to God first. He believed God created the world and guided it according to His will. He viewed science as merely another way to learn more about God's creation. Robert said, "From a knowledge of His work, we shall know Him."

Robert believed a scientist should have knowledge in all fields, including the Bible. He learned Latin, Greek, Hebrew and other biblical languages to better understand the Word of God.

One of his best known religious books is *Occasional Reflections*. He wrote the book while living the solitary life at Stalbridge. It is a collection of Christian devotions. The book showed Robert Boyle's writing at its best.

While living at Stalbridge, Robert also wrote *The Martyrdom of Theodora and Didymus*. The story is about the young and beautiful Theodora and the soldier she intended to marry. Both were Christians. Their exciting story is set in ancient Rome. Robert used plenty of action and adventure to tell how Didymus rescued Theodora from slavery before a pagan god. The book passed from person to person in handwritten form before finally appearing in print. The story was the first religious romance ever written.

Robert Boyle became intensely interested in worldwide evangelism. He never cared for fame or public office. However, his missionary enthusiasm led him to serve as governor of the Corporation for the Propagation of the Gospel. He also accepted a position with the East India Company. He used these positions to help spread the Gospel in many countries.

He often spoke to others about his faith. He spent much of his own money for translations of the Bible in other languages. He gave away thousands of the Bibles.

People who knew Robert Boyle often remarked upon his gentle, honest and peaceful nature. He never let vanity, envy or anger trouble him. Even when people violently disagreed with him, he didn't stoop to angry words or insults.

He was a foe of religious intolerance. People who

disagreed with the established religion often faced persecution. Robert worked quietly and behind the scenes to help subjects of injustice. He gave generously to poor people and to victims of natural disasters. Those he helped often never learned his name.

Although Robert Boyle became famous and wealthy, he remained a humble Christian. Throughout his life, he read the Bible each morning, overcoming illness, eye trouble and the press of other duties.

Robert Boyle died on December 30, 1691. In his will he provided for a series of lectures, not on science, but on the defense of Christianity against unbelievers. These sermons are known as the Boyle lectures. Robert started them to promote the fact that in the study of nature scientists can find much evidence that God created the universe.

Today, Robert Boyle is remembered for his discovery of Boyle's law, for making chemistry into a true science, and as a founder of the Royal Society. He was a man of many talents and one of the first modern scientists. He should also be remembered as a Christian who never wavered in his strong commitment to God.

# BIBLIOGRAPHY

E. N. Da C. Andrade, *A brief History of the Royal Society* (London: The Royal Society, 1960).

Isaac Asimov, *Asimov's Biographical Encyclopedia of Science and Technology*, second revised edition (Garden City: Doubleday & Company, Inc., 1982).

Thomas Birch, Editor, *Robert Boyle, The Works* (Hildesheim, Germany: Georg Olms Verlagsbuchhandlung, 1965). Reproduction of the six volume London edition of 1772 with an introduction by Douglas McKie.

Robert Boyle, *The Sceptical Chemist* (NY: E. P. Dutton Company, Inc., 1911).

L. M. Cullen, *Life in Ireland* (NY: G. P. Putnam's Sons, 1968).

John F. Fulton, *A Bibliography of the Honourable Robert Boyle*, second edition (Oxford: Claredon Press, 1961).

Marie Boas Hall, *Robert Boyle on Natural Philosophy* (Westport, CT: Congressional Information Service, Inc., 1980). Reprint of the edition published by Indiana University Press, Bloomington, 1965.

Flora Masson, *Robert Boyle* (London: Constable & Company Ltd., 1914).

Louis Trenchard More, *The Life and Works of the Honourable Robert Boyle* (NY: Oxford University Press, 1944).

Henry M. Morris, *Men of Science, Men of God* (San Diego: Creation-Life Publishers, 1982).

J. R. Partington, *A Short History of Chemistry*, third edition (NY: Harper & Brothers, 1957).

Robert Pilkington, *Robert Boyle* (London: John Murray, 1959).

Ernest Rhys, Editor, *The Diary of Samuel Pepys* (NY: E. P. Dutton & Co., 1906).

Harry Sootin, *Robert Boyle* (NY: Franklin Watts, Inc., 1962).

Grant Uden, *They Looked Like This* (Oxford: Basil Blackwell, 1965).

Rosemary Weir, *The Man Who Built a City* (NY: Farrar, Straus & Giroux, 1971).

# INDEX